Just What War Is

JUST WHAT WAR IS

The Civil War Writings of De Forest and Bierce

Michael W. Schaefer

The University of Tennessee Press / Knoxville

Copyright © 1997 by The University of Tennessee Press / Knoxville.
All Rights Reserved. Manufactured in the United States of America.
First Edition.

Excerpts from *The Things They Carried*. Copyright © by Tim O'Brien. Reprinted by permission of Houghton Mifflin Co./Seymour Lawrence. All rights reserved.

Excerpts from *The Face of Battle* by John Keegan. Copyright © 1976 by John Keegan. Used by permission of Viking Penguin, a division of Penguin Books USA Inc.

The paper in this book meets the minimum requirements of the American National Standard for Permanence of Paper for Printed Library Materials. The binding materials have been chosen for strength and durability. Printed on recycled paper.

Library of Congress Cataloging-in-Publication Data

Schaefer, Michael W., 1951–
Just what war is : the Civil War writings of De Forest
    and Bierce / Michael W. Schaefer. — 1st ed.
       p. cm.
    Includes bibliographical references and index.
    ISBN 0-87049-941-6 (cl.: alk. paper)
    1. American fiction—19th century—History and criticism. 2. United States—History—Civil War, 1861–1865—Literature and the war. 3. War stories, American—History and criticism. 4. De Forest, John William, 1826–1906—Knowledge—War. 5. Bierce, Ambrose, 1842–1914?—Knowledge—War. 6. United States—History—Civil War, 1861–1865—Historiography. 7. Realism in literature. 8. Combat in literature. 9. War in literature. I. Title.
    PS374.C53S33 1997
    813'.309358—dc21   97-4898

Contents

Acknowledgments	vii
Introduction	ix
PART I. UNDER FIRE: THE COMPONENTS OF REALISM IN COMBAT WRITING	
1. What the Soldier Does in Combat	3
2. What the Soldier Feels in Combat	8
3. The Soldier's Experience in De Forest and Bierce	15
PART II. JOHN W. DE FOREST	
4. The Limits of Experience	23
5. The Uses of Influence	42
PART III. AMBROSE BIERCE	
6. The Failures of History	65
7. To March toward the Sound of the Guns	103
Conclusion: "I Would Not Have Missed This for Any Consideration"	131
Notes	141
Works Cited	159
Index	167

Acknowledgments

The flaws in this book are all mine; however, I share with many others the credit for whatever is valuable in it. I owe an enormous debt to Richard D. Rust, who, as my dissertation director at the University of North Carolina at Chapel Hill, expertly supervised the original version of this work and also provided insightful commentary on a later draft. Everett Emerson, Howard Harper, and Christopher Armitage of the University of North Carolina likewise gave generously of their time and expertise as readers; I am especially grateful to Professor Armitage for steering me to relevant material in Wilfred Owen's letters. Valuable advice on subsequent drafts came from Joseph Cox, of the United States Military Academy, and Donald Anderson, of the United States Air Force Academy. At the University of Tennessee Press, I am indebted to Meredith Morris-Babb, Stan Ivester, and Karin Kaufman, whose keen eyes have improved my work in a number of ways. Thanks are also due to Randal Allred, of Brigham

Young University–Hawaii, and Ian King, of Hendrix College, for provocative suggestions on further research, as well as to John Limon and Timothy Sweet, whose writings on the Civil War stimulated my own thinking and, more specifically, guided me to pertinent material in the works of Homer, Walt Whitman, Roland Barthes, Paul de Man, and Fredric Jameson.

I owe gratitude of a different sort but an equal magnitude to my colleagues at the University of Central Arkansas. Terrance Kearns, my department chair, and Gary Stark, my dean, provided many kinds of support, including the sabbatical leave that enabled me to complete this project. Robert Lowrey made sure that my manuscript went to the right press. Henry N. Rogers III, Conrad Shumaker, James Fowler, Raymond-Jean Frontain, Rebecca Williams, Charlene Bland, Barbara Stanley, Gary Davenport, Richard Gaughan, Linda Arnold, John Lammers, Phillip Anderson, Frances Jeffery, and Wayne and Ellen Stengel provided counsel and sanity on a daily basis, as did Joseph Lombardi, of Hendrix College.

My profoundest appreciation goes to my wife, Lynn, whose nurture and good humor never fail.

This book is dedicated to the memory of the three people to whom I owe the greatest debts of all: Cyril M. Schaefer, Jimmie Lou Schaefer, and Robert Bain.

Introduction

At the beginning of his short story "War Memories," Stephen Crane addresses the difficulties a writer faces in trying to convey accurately to a reader the experience of battle. "'But to get the real thing!'" says the story's protagonist, Vernall, an American war correspondent modeled closely on Crane himself, as he sets out for Cuba to cover the Spanish-American War. "'It seems impossible, because war is neither magnificent nor squalid; it is simply life, and an expression of life can always evade us. We can never tell life, one to another, although sometimes we think we can'" (222).

By either direct statement or implication, a number of American writers of the generation preceding Crane's, veterans of the Civil War, bear out this assessment of the writer's limited ability to express the reality of life at war; probably the most famous formulation of this problem is Walt Whitman's assertion that "the real war will never get in the books" (112).[1]

Nevertheless, many of these men—including Ambrose Bierce, Joseph Kirkland, Sidney Lanier, James Kendall Hosmer, John William De Forest, Wilbur F. Hinman, and S. Weir Mitchell—attempted to create their versions of "the real thing," based on their own combat experiences, in memoirs, novels, and stories about the war. All these works have their merits, but those of two former Union officers, De Forest and Bierce, stand out as the most successful; as Wayne Miller notes, they are among the very few who "established a new criterion for judging a writer's performance in regard to the treatment of war: how close does he get to the way it was?" (89).[2] Exploring the full meaning of this statement—what we can know about "the way it was" and how we can judge De Forest's and Bierce's success in conveying those circumstances—is the purpose of this study.

The concept of "realism" as a literary term is crucial to such an explanation, for the earlier of this pair to publish writings drawn from his personal experience of combat, De Forest, explicitly wanted to correct mistaken notions that he believed many journalists, historians, and fiction writers had propagated about battle. Just as his friend William Dean Howells sought to eliminate romanticized falsehoods from other areas of life as represented in fiction, De Forest campaigned vigorously for writers to come forth with the firsthand truth about battle. Regarding customary depictions of battle, he notes wryly in his memoirs that in his first engagement "I had a sabre and revolver all ready, for of course I expected a severe hand-to-hand struggle; not having yet learned that bayonet fighting occurs mainly in newspapers and other works of fiction" (*Volunteer's Adventures* 66). De Forest's Civil War works are full of such acerbic asides about inaccurate representations of combat, but his fullest treatment of battle writing is an 1879 *Atlantic Monthly* article entitled "Our Military Past and Future." Reviewing a number of military histories he finds inadequate as pictures of combat, De Forest asserts that much battle writing consists of a standardized set of vivid turns of phrase, which he terms "rhetorical generalities" (572), that create excitement but reveal little about what actually happens during a clash of arms. In response, he calls for accurate, detailed accounts to offset "the trashy, misleading ones which prattle of 'billows of cavalry' and 'infantry standing like rocks.'" He wants "not such stuff as the world has had about war from a host of ignorant romancers calling themselves historians; but books which show just what war is, and what to do amidst its difficulties and perplexities" (572).

More recently, English historian John Keegan has similarly addressed the inadequacies of most military histories as realistic depictions of combat. His principal work on the subject, *The Face of Battle,* is worth examining at some length for its detailed criticism of the kind of nineteenth-century works De Forest has in mind in his *Atlantic* essay. As an example of the sort of imprecise, romanticized account that both De Forest and Keegan dismiss as "the battle-piece," Keegan offers a passage from General Sir William Napier's 1840 *History of the War in the Peninsula,* an examination of the British army's campaigns from 1808 to 1814 against Napoleon's forces in Spain and Portugal. This excerpt, which Keegan notes is "one of the most frequently quoted of all descriptive accounts of the British army's battles in the Peninsula and a firm favourite with compilers of military anthologies" (38), describes the critical moment of the battle of Albuera (16 May 1811), an attack uphill by the British Fusilier Brigade that broke the main French battle line. When the Fusiliers began their advance, Napier says,

> Such a gallant line, issuing from the midst of the smoke and rapidly separating itself from the confused and broken multitude [of the rest of the British force], startled the enemy's masses, then augmenting and pressing forward as to an assured victory: they wavered, hesitated, and, vomiting forth a storm of fire, hastily endeavoured to enlarge their front, while a fearful discharge of grape from all their artillery whistled through the British ranks. Myers [the Fusilier Brigade commander] was killed, Cole, the three colonels, Ellis, Blakeney, and Hawkshawe [the four officers directly below Myers in the chain of command], fell wounded, and the fusilier battalions, struck by the iron tempest, reeled and staggered like sinking ships. But suddenly and sternly recovering, they closed on their terrible enemies, and then was seen with what strength and majesty the British soldier fights. In vain did Soult [the French commander] with voice and gesture animate the Frenchmen; in vain did the hardiest veterans, breaking from the crowded columns, sacrifice their lives to gain time for the mass to open out on such a

fair field; in vain did the mass itself bear up, and fiercely striving fire indiscriminately upon friends and foes, while the horsemen hovering on the flank threatened to charge the advancing line. Nothing could stop that astonishing infantry. No sudden burst of undisciplined valour, no nervous enthusiasm weakened the stability of their order, their flashing eyes were bent on the dark columns in their front, their measured tread shook the ground, their dreadful volleys swept away the head of every formation, their deafening shouts overpowered the dissonant cries that broke from all parts of the tumultuous crowd, as slowly and with a horrid carnage it was pushed by the incessant vigour of the attack to the farthest edge of the height. There the French reserve, mixing with the struggling multitude, endeavoured to restore the fight but only augmented the irremediable disorder, and the mighty mass giving way like a loosened cliff, went headlong down the steep: the rain flowed after in streams discoloured with blood, and eighteen hundred unwounded men, the remnant of six thousand unconquerable British soldiers, stood triumphant on the fatal hill. (Qtd. in Keegan 37–38)

"Now as Romantic prose passages go," Keegan begins his critique, "this is clearly a very remarkable achievement, rich in imagery, thunderous in rhythm and immensely powerful in emotional effect; it almost vibrates on the page, towards its climax threatens indeed to loosen the reader's hold on the book" (38). He then points out, however, that many of the elements that create this power—hyperbole such as "their measured tread shook the ground," standard similes such as "reeled and staggered like sinking ships," visual and aural effects such as "vomiting forth a storm of fire," "streams discoloured with blood," "deafening shouts" and "dissonant cries"—tell a reader nothing about what the Fusiliers actually *did*. Keegan's first specific complaint is with Napier's depiction of the soldiers as behaving uniformly. "Am I alone in wondering," Keegan asks, "whether a body of men, admittedly trained soldiers, but of whom two out of three were to suffer wounds or death as a consequence of their acts, really advanced uphill under heavy fire without once showing 'nervous enthusiasm' or indeed anything but 'disciplined valour'?" (38). In Napier's narrative, the soldiers of both sides demonstrate no individuality: "[T]he British are all attacking and all with equal intensity . . . [while] the French likewise are all resisting. . . . [N]o individual turns tail and runs, drops down to sham dead, or stands thunder-struck at the indescribable horror of it all" (39).

Keegan's second criticism is that Napier fails to provide any clear explanation of the reasons for the attack's success. The Fusilier Brigade alone assaults a far larger enemy force composed of infantry, cavalry, and artillery and commanded by one of the finest soldiers of the period. Soon the brigade is leaderless and sustains a two-thirds casualty rate, yet it completes its advance and drives the French from the field. Napier, Keegan points out, offers no comprehensible description of how the Fusiliers accomplish this feat; citing the piece's "abrupt, indeed quite discontinuous movement" (39), Keegan notes that all Napier says in the way of cause and effect is that "the British advance, they and the French exchange volleys, 'carnage' ensues, and then suddenly the French are over the steep" (39). How, Keegan asks, are the French forced over the steep—by the press of superior numbers, by hand-to-hand fighting, by the points of British bayonets, by an outbreak of panic in their ranks? The reader consulting Napier for the answer will never know. Napier ignores even the most elementary questions about the attack: what effect the dead and wounded have on its progress and what happens to those dead and wounded as it proceeds. As Keegan explains,

> Men advancing in close order across a constricted space against an enemy with whom they exchange effective fire will have to step over the bodies first of their own dead and wounded comrades, then over those of the enemy; would not that have interrupted . . . the Fusiliers' "measured tread"? And what did the wounded—combatant beings no longer but none the less, indeed perhaps all the more, sentient for that—do with themselves while the struggle raged round them? In Napier's account, the dead and wounded apparently dematerialize as soon as struck down. (40)

Clearly, despite its power as prose, Napier's account does not show "just what war is"—a result, in the words of an anonymous contemporary critic, of Napier's tendency to sacrifice "to the general grand effect all minor and apparently trifling things" (qtd. in Keegan 41).

In refusing to sacrifice such "trifles" as cause and effect and human behavior, De Forest and Bierce, anticipating Keegan by a century, seek to develop in their memoirs and fiction a more accurately descriptive, more realistic form of combat discourse. Speaking usually from the viewpoint of those directly involved in the fighting as opposed to that of the generals who oversee it from some distance, they deny Napier's underlying assumption that the experience of battle consists of the participant's seeing armies maneuvering smoothly and uniformly on broad plains and his consciously pitting his society's ideology against the enemy's.[3] Instead, in these men's works the individual soldier in battle sees only his own unit and perhaps one or two others in a clearing amid dense woods or on an otherwise eerily empty field. He has little idea where the rest of his army is and what it is doing; all he knows of strategy and tactics is that the enemy may emerge from any direction at any moment. If the enemy does appear, the soldier gives little thought to the cause for which he is ostensibly fighting. He uses his weapons not to free the slaves or defend states' rights or advance any other high purpose but simply to keep from being killed. Moreover, such conflict is seldom composed of massed volleys and charges concluding with sword and bayonet fighting; each side usually advances or retreats slowly and piecemeal, firing from whatever cover is available and rarely getting close enough to the other for hand-to-hand combat.

If De Forest and Bierce thus agree on what battle is and what the soldier does in it, to a large extent they also concur on how he feels in its midst. Primarily, he feels frightened. If he is new to battle, he may respond to that fear by fleeing. If he has been effectively trained and is well led, however, he is more likely to master this fear, through a recognition that standing to face the enemy is actually safer than turning his unprotected back in flight and through his sense of community with the other men in his company or regiment. These realizations mark the metamorphosis of an untested recruit into a veteran soldier.

This list of similarities in De Forest's and Bierce's work leads to an obvious question regarding their efforts to provide a realistic picture of combat. We know what they say battle is like, but how can we be sure that their assertions are accurate, that they do in fact provide a more realistic picture of warfare than the battle-piece rhetoricians? One way might be simply to point to the uniformity of their observations; since both writers say much the same thing, their assertions would appear to contain a core of common truth. But verifying their observations in this manner, without reference to a larger context, is not entirely persuasive. A better way is to supply that context by examining a number of other, nonfiction sources. As we will see, both general studies of warfare and accounts of combat in the Civil War in particular accord with De Forest's and Bierce's depictions.

Part I

UNDER FIRE

The Components of Realism in Combat Writing

CHAPTER 1

What the Soldier Does in Combat

In *Acts of War,* a wide-ranging survey of men's experiences in battle, Richard Holmes takes up the issue of the soldier's limited view of his surroundings in combat. "The battlefield," he notes, "given colour and texture by the rich palette of artists, writers, and film-makers, is . . . empty and drab to many of those who live upon it. It is sometimes so unspectacular that it may not even be identifiable as a battlefield" (150). Discussing nineteenth-century painters' representations of battles, which were as tightly bound by vivid but inaccurate conventions as many of that era's fictional and historical depictions, Holmes says that "the busy canvases of battles all too often reflected what the artist wished to believe had taken place rather than what had actually happened. . . . The crammed canvases of most nineteenth-century military painters fail to reflect a battlefield which was, in the participants' view, more often empty than crowded" (61–63).

If the nineteenth-century battlefield thus offered little for the average soldier to see, the conditions of combat made impossible a clear view of even that little. In addition to misrepresenting the battlefield's emptiness, Holmes points out, nineteenth-century military painters "do not do justice to the clouds of thick powder-smoke which . . . often reduced observation to a few yards. Captain Cavalie Mercer, commanding a battery at Waterloo, was in the very forefront of the battle. But he saw little of it. 'What was passing to the right and left of us I know no more than the man in the moon,' he wrote. 'The smoke confined our vision to a very small compass, so that my battle was restricted to the two squares [of infantry] and my own battery'" (63).

Such limited sight logically suggests concomitant limitations on the soldier's grasp of the battle's overall shape and purposes, and most realistic histories of combat—that is, those not partaking of the "battle-piece" format—are as unequivocal on this matter as their fictional counterparts. The writers of such histories offer two reasons for this ignorance beyond the restrictions of the soldier's literal sight line. The more obvious of these is that the typical enlisted man or low-level officer is simply not privy to a broad understanding of his strategic situation. "Even when a man can see a good deal of what is going on around him," Holmes says, "he is unlikely to be able to remember it accurately or to put his recollections into context. The reasons for this stem as much from the organisation of armies as they do from the workings of the human brain. It is only in the comparatively recent past [well after the era of the American Civil War] that the average soldier was likely to see—or to understand—a map, or to be given a glimpse of the broad strategic picture by a verbal briefing or printed news sheet" (152).

Beyond this bureaucratic limitation on his understanding is the more personal impediment that for the average soldier, as Keegan notes, the experience of combat "takes place in a wildly unstable physical and emotional environment" that is scarcely conducive to broad or even localized strategic reflection. If the general's view, from which the battle-piece is usually written, is of "large, intellectually manageable blocks of human beings going here or there and doing, or failing to do, as he directs," the soldier's view, "like that of all human beings confronted with the threat or reality of extreme personal danger . . . will center on the issue of personal survival" (47).

A natural corollary to this simple focus on survival is the soldier's lack of concern with ideology in the heat of combat. Many writers have at one time or another suggested that a soldier's devotion to his cause is the primary force in keeping his fear for himself at bay on the battlefield, but most reports of veterans' experiences fail to bear this notion out. What veterans emphasize, rather, is that the soldier's concern for personal survival is normally subsumed into an overriding concentration on the mechanics pressingly at hand: loading, aiming, firing. In short, rather than overcoming his fears through an awareness of his cause's rightness, the soldier usually finds himself too preoccupied on a practical level to give in to his trepidations. Gathering material for his 1943 book *Fear in Battle,* John Dollard questioned three hundred veterans of the Abraham Lincoln Brigade, an American volunteer unit that served with the Loyalist army in the Spanish Civil War, about the most important factors in overcoming their battlefield fears. Most mentioned a belief in their side's aims and a strong antipathy to the other side's, but they indicated that these feelings were more important before and after a battle than as it took place. Eighty-four percent of his interviewees, Dollard says, reported that they felt themselves better soldiers for "concentrating on each step of a task when in the presence of danger" (42). This statistic leads him to the conclusion that "the soldier in battle is not forever whispering, 'My cause, my cause.' He is too busy for that. Ideology functions *before* battle, to get the man in; and *after* battle by blocking thoughts of escape" (56).[1]

If combat historians and psychologists agree on the nature of the individual soldier's experience in combat, they are in equal accord concerning the larger picture. They unanimously represent battle—especially Civil War battle—as a series of piecemeal movements forward and back that only rarely develop into hand-to-hand encounters, rather than as a set of massed charges concluding with the clash of bayonets. Such charges were in fact relatively common early in the Civil War, but, as Gerald Linderman points out in *Embattled Courage,* a study of the average Civil War soldier's experience in the field, technological advancement gradually changed the nature of combat. Most high-ranking Civil War officers, Linderman explains, had developed their understanding of tactics during the Mexican War, a period when the standard soldier's weapon was a single-shot, muzzle-loading, smoothbore musket. Because this weapon had an effective range of only about one hundred yards and required at least thirty seconds to reload, a massed charge stood a considerable chance of success; a defending force would be likely to get off only one volley before the attackers closed with them hand to hand and used the momentum of the charge to break the defensive line. American forces repeatedly won battles during the Mexican War by employing such bayonet charges, and initially Civil War commanders saw no reason that this tactical maneuver would not work as well against their new enemy. In the fifteen years between the Mexican and the Civil Wars, however, weapons had changed in a way that shifted the advantage from the offense to the defense in this kind of assault. The soldier's standard issue was still a single-shot, muzzle-loading musket, but now this weapon had a rifled barrel—that is, its barrel was grooved in such a way that a bullet would spin as it was fired. This modification increased the musket's effective range to nearly four hundred yards; thus, a defending force could fire at a charging line from a much greater distance and so get off several volleys at least, exacting a far higher toll and making the cost of a charge much more daunting for both the men involved in it and the commander directing it. Linderman notes that "[e]ven with the persistence of poor firing instruction and wretched firing discipline, rifling strengthened the hand of the defense decisively" (135). The result was that "Civil War soldiers increasingly realized the assault's inefficacy, and not all remained inert in the face of its failure. As the war pressed on, a tendency appeared, provenance unknown, toward tactical variation. Attacks in massed column became less frequent, yielding to open formations supplemented by far greater numbers of skirmishers. Assaults sustained until victory or defeat gave way to advances by rushes, with the men resorting to cover" wherever it became available (138).

Linderman backs this explanation with reports from combatants who themselves noted this tactical evolution and, like De Forest, soon realized that bayonet engagements took place more often in newspapers than on battlefields. One such soldier was Asa W. Bartlett, author of the *History of the Twelfth Regiment, New Hampshire Volunteers in the War of the Rebellion* (Concord: I. C. Evans, 1897). Attempting its first massed charge at Chancellorsville, this regiment quickly lost four hundred of its five hundred men. This "terrible experience," Bartlett reports, "taught [the survivors] a lesson that each one is now practicing; for every man has his tree behind which he is fighting" (qtd. in Linderman 138).

Other Civil War historians' findings also support Linderman's assertions. Likewise explaining that the rifled musket's improved range made massed bayonet charges excessively dangerous, Champ Clark in *Decoying the Yanks,* a study of Stonewall Jackson's Shenandoah Valley campaign, notes that "during a three-month period that included six major battles, Federal surgeons treated a scant 37 bayonet wounds" (40). The bayonet's casualty ratio for the entire war proved similarly low. According to James I. Robertson Jr., although 94 percent of all those wounded during the war were hit by rifle or pistol fire and 5.5 percent were struck by artillery, only .5 percent fell victim to bayonets and sabers (*Tenting* 88).[2]

CHAPTER 2

What the Soldier Feels in Combat

With the physical circumstances of battle established, we now move to its psychological effects on participants. The conventional wisdom is that the soldier gradually becomes inured to the stresses of combat, a notion veterans themselves sometimes foster. In his characteristically colorful vein, General George Patton once observed that "[b]attle is far less frightening than those of you who have not been in it are apt to think.... All this bull about thinking of your mother and your sweetheart, and your wives ... is overemphasized by writers who describe battles not as they are but as writers who have never heard a hostile shot or missed a meal think they are" (qtd. in Keegan and Holmes, *Soldiers* 262).

Patton speaks here from the viewpoint of a commander; we may legitimately question whether his observation holds true for the lower-level soldier. All historians who have thoroughly studied line infantrymen's experiences under fire have found that battle *is* indeed tremendously frightening and remains so despite the soldier's length of frontline service. American World War II combat historian S. L. A. Marshall addresses this issue emphatically. "It is a matter commonly noted," he says,

> that they who write of war tend to use loosely the expression "battle-seasoned troops" as if there were a kind of mental toughening which comes from experience under fire.
>
> The idea is wholly misleading; it mistakes the shadow for the substance. One of the effects of the shock of engagement is that it shakes the weakest files out of the organization. But as for the veterans who remain, they do not grow more callous to danger as they meet it increasingly nor do they ever become more eager for the contest. As they grow in knowledge, the nerve may become steadier in that they are less susceptible to wild imaginings. But if it were certain that battle experience of itself provided the sure safeguard against this evil, then it could not happen that high commanders sometimes fail in crisis because of it. (123)[1]

The soldier does not discard his fears, then, but learns to cope with them. And according to Marshall and other historians, men of all armies in all eras cope with their fears through the same four-step progression.

Initially, before and during the soldier's first engagement, his fear is of fear itself; not yet knowing how he will behave under fire, the apprehension that he may disgrace himself by running is uppermost in his mind. Dollard's research bears out this fact: "fear of being a coward" was the concern that weighed most heavily on his interviewees before their first engagement (28). Holmes gives perhaps the most lucid explanation of this phenomenon, drawing on psychiatrists' and other historians' findings:

> Freud distinguished between what he termed "objective anxiety," or fear stemming from a genuine and identifiable threat, and "neurotic anxiety," based upon a conflict between instinct and conscience. There is a learned dispute among psychologists as to whether or not anxiety serves to signal danger to an individual and, in so doing, to provoke a response: Freud argued that it did. What is clear, however, is that apprehension—while not necessarily synonymous with neurotic

anxiety—does involve a struggle between the demands of the instinct and the dictates of conscience. This is especially true before a soldier's first battle, when his apprehension focuses upon the conflict between an instinctive prompting to seek safety and a desire not to deviate from the standards expected of him by his leaders and comrades. (141)

Under usual circumstances, however, this fear soon gives way to the second stage: the soldier holds his place, bolstered by the example of his officers' courage, by the threat of punishment at their hands should he flee (or, if he is an officer, by the need to set the example of courage), and above all by his desire not to let down or disgrace himself before his peers and friends. "Wherever one surveys the forces of the battlefield," Marshall points out, "it is to see that fear is general among men, but to observe further that men commonly are loath that their fear will be expressed in specific acts which their comrades will recognize as cowardice. The majority are unwilling to take extraordinary risks and do not aspire to a hero's role, but they are equally unwilling that they should be considered the least worthy among those present" (149).

With his self-generated fears thus mastered, the soldier finds himself at the third stage, which may occur almost immediately after the second or be delayed until a subsequent battle. As the euphoria at discovering he is not a coward wears off, the man under fire attains a clearer understanding of what is going on outside himself and thus becomes more aware of the physical dangers he is in, whereas previously he perceived these only dimly beneath his fears about his courage. The realization that he is in more imminent danger of death or maiming than of social or psychological disgrace sets up a new round of fear that, given its more rational basis in observable fact, can never be entirely mastered—or, as Marshall says, to which the veteran does not grow more callous. "A soldier who is unfamiliar with battle," Holmes notes, "may invest combat with far more alarming characteristics than it turns out to possess, and may, as is so often the case, be surprised to discover how well he copes with it. But an experienced soldier, whose threat appraisal is based upon considerable objective evidence, may sustain as much stress in a relatively minor action late in his career as he did in his first battle" (140).

Dollard and his statistics bear Marshall and Holmes out on this point;

before their first battle only 25 percent of his subjects were most fearful of being seriously wounded, but for subsequent engagements this figure rose to 39 percent (28). Even more decisive proof of the continued presence of fear comes from the belief held by Dollard's interviewees that, rather than being hardened to combat through repeated exposure to it, many soldiers possess only a finite amount of courage that combat gradually exhausts. "The men indicate in their comments," Dollard notes, "that a soldier may have just so many battles in him and after he goes through these he should be treated indulgently if he breaks" (48).

If this discovery of the true nature of battlefield fear is the initial step toward veteranship, the fourth phase marks the soldier's final passage into that state. Recognizing the danger he is in, the soldier masters his irrational, primal instinct for flight and comes to the counterintuitive realization that his chances of death or injury are greatest when he turns his back to the enemy. His safety is most assured—as assured as it can be in his fundamentally unsafe environment—when he continues to fight in the hopes of removing the threat to his safety. This realization made itself apparent as soon as studies of the line soldier's psychology began in the mid-nineteenth century. The pioneer in this field was Ardant du Picq, a French infantry officer who had seen combat in the Crimea and Algeria and subsequently embarked on the first large-scale, systematic, firsthand study of battle psychology. What he learned, as John Keegan summarizes it, was that

> soldiers die in greatest numbers when they run, because it is when they turn their backs to the enemy that they are least able to defend themselves. It is their rational acceptance of the danger of running that makes civilized soldiers so formidable, he [du Picq] says, that and the discipline which has them in its bonds. And by discipline he does not mean the operation of an abstract principle but the example and sanctions exercised by the officers of an organized force. Men fight, he says in short, from fear: fear of the consequences first of not fighting (i.e. punishment), then of not fighting well (i.e. slaughter). (71)

Almost every memoir penned by a Civil War soldier either overtly or implicitly bears out du Picq's insights. Such men nearly invariably find fear omnipresent on the battlefield; as Keegan notes, the Civil War "had already produced, by the outbreak of the First World War, a remarkable crop of soldiers' literature, in which battle had been depicted very much from the private's rather than the general's angle of vision, and many of the authors had not disguised how frightened they had been" (71). But along with fear, most such writers discuss their discovery of the rational response to it. John Haley, a Maine volunteer, explains in just these terms his regiment's method of coping with imminent danger during the second day of Gettysburg. Defending a stone wall against a considerably larger Confederate force, Haley says, he and his veteran comrades, carefully observing the realities of their situation along with its dangers, found continued defense more practical than retreat, even when a retreat was ordered. "I'm confident," Haley writes,

> that we could have held a reasonable force [of Confederates] at bay, but they were strongly reinforced. Our ammunition now began to run low and the [Union] troops on our right, being flanked, gave way, exposing us to a heavy flank fire. The troops who gave way had only a rail fence in front of them, while we had a stone wall, which sheltered us well until our flank was uncovered. Even then we didn't hurry about leaving. The batteries in our rear still continued to pour destruction into the Rebel ranks, and it seemed nothing short of annihilation would stop them.
>
> At this point, while shot, shell, spherical case, and cannister filled the air, General de Trobriand, our brigade commander, rode down into the wheat field and inquired, "What troops are those holding the stone wall so stubbornly?" On learning it was the 17th Maine, one of his regiments, he ordered us to "Fall back, right away!" But we didn't *hear* the order. It isn't often that an order to fall back in a battlefield is disregarded. The old fellow didn't quite comprehend this state of ours. We had good reason for our action. This stone wall was a great protection and the Rebels were straining every nerve to get it for the same purpose. So, we held it till our ammunition was exhausted and we had used all we could find on the dead and wounded. If we could hold on until reinforcements or a supply of ammunition came, all would be well. Otherwise, no one could tell what direful woes might befall us. (101)

Haley's use of the first-person plural also reveals a second and equally important aspect of veteranship, one absolutely necessary to the action of the first: the soldier's sense of community with the other members of his unit. Marshall explains that, despite du Picq's and other historians' emphasis on officers' imposition of discipline, the average soldier's rational understanding of continued fighting as the safest response to danger can only come into play when the soldier is calmed by the close presence of others about whose welfare he cares and by whom he feels that care reciprocated. Such feelings lead to the unity of purpose Haley's regiment displayed at the stone wall. "Since troops do not conquer the fear of death and wounds," Marshall asserts,

> it is idle to think of any such basis for the establishment of combat discipline. The latter is simply the reflection of the growth of unit confidence which comes of increased awareness and utilization of one's own resources under conditions which at first seem extraordinary but gradually become familiar.
>
> Until that kind of confidence is born, there can be no effective action. Green troops are more likely to flee the field than others only because they have not learned to think and act together. Individually, they may be as brave and willing then as during any subsequent period, but individual bravery and willingness will not stand against organized shock.
>
> With the growth of experience troops learn to apply the lessons of contact and communicating, and out of these things comes the tactical cohesion which enables a group of individuals to make the most of their united strength and stand steady in the face of sudden emergency. (124)

In units in which this necessary fellow-feeling has been fostered by officers and men alike, even the soldier new to battle is likely to stand and fight. "That his own outfit is grouped around him is enough," says Marshall. "[E]very man is in aid in helping him choke down the fear which might otherwise have stopped him" (47). Failing such cohesion, however, the soldier's individual instinct for self-preservation will take over, even in the case of the veteran. Marshall explains that

[t]he seeds of panic are always present in troops so long as they are in the midst of physical danger, the form of which changes from moment to moment. In the majority of men the retention of self-discipline under the conditions of the battlefield depends upon the maintaining of an appearance of discipline within the unit. Should the latter begin to dissolve, only a small minority of the most hardy individuals will retain self-control. The others cannot stand fast if the circumstances appear to justify flight. When other men flee, the social pressure is lifted and the average soldier will respond as if he had been given a release from duty, for he knows that his personal failure is made inconspicuous by the general dissolution. . . .

It is therefore to be noted as a principle that, all other things being equal, the tactical unity of men working together in combat will be in the ratio of their knowledge and sympathetic understanding of each other. Lacking these things, though they be well-trained soldiers, they are not likely to adhere unless danger has so surrounded them that they must do so in order to survive, and even then, quick surrender is the more probable result. (149–50)

CHAPTER 3

The Soldier's Experience in De Forest and Bierce

As the nonfictional analogues examined in the preceding two chapters bear out, the works of De Forest and Bierce do offer in their memoirs and fictionalized renderings of battle, as those were described in the opening pages of this study, a truthful account of what the Civil War soldier did and felt. In terms of simply accurately noting the most common events and feelings generated by and in the moment of combat, both writers capture Crane's "real thing," life as it is. Indeed, even many incidents in their fiction that at first glance appear either too perfectly ironic or too bizarre to be anything but inventions prove on closer inspection to correspond to actual reports of combat. One such example appears in De Forest's Civil War novel, *Miss Ravenel's Conversion from Secession to Loyalty*. De Forest devotes a part of this story to the Union siege of Port Hudson, Louisiana, in 1863; at one point during the six weeks of this engagement he offers a scene in which a Union soldier, believing himself safe behind the lines, is just raising a mug of beer to his lips when he is killed by a Confederate sniper. Despite the too-pat quality of this circumstance—its precise ironic comment on the notion of a man's being in most danger in war when he feels safest and most relaxed—this event actually occurred, as De Forest reports in his account of his own real-life participation in the operations at Port Hudson, which occupies two chapters in his volume of wartime reminiscences, *A Volunteer's Adventures.*

An example on a larger scale appears in Bierce's short story "Chickamauga." In one of the most famous scenes in Civil War fiction, the deaf-mute boy who is the protagonist of the story observes what appears to be a landscape in motion that on closer inspection proves, horrifyingly, to be composed of crawling wounded men:

> They crept upon their hands and knees. They used their hands only, dragging their legs. They used their knees only, their arms hanging idle at their sides. They strove to rise to their feet, but fell prone in the attempt. They did nothing naturally, and nothing alike, save only to advance foot by foot in the same direction. Singly, in pairs and in little groups, they came on through the gloom, some halting now and again while others crept slowly past them, then resuming their movement. They came by dozens and by hundreds; as far on either hand as one could see in the deepening gloom they extended and the black wood behind them appeared to be inexhaustible. . . . Occasionally one who had paused did not again go on, but lay motionless. He was dead. Some, pausing, made strange gestures with their hands, erected their arms and lowered them again, clasped their heads; spread palms upward, as men are sometimes seen to do in public prayer. (102)

This vision seems at first glance a typical product of Bierce's macabre imagination, but such sights were in fact frequent after battles. Many veterans described them in their memoirs, a prime instance being a recollection by William Averell, a colonel in the Federal cavalry who commanded the Army of the Potomac's rear guard following the battle of Malvern Hill, fought on 1 July 1862. All that night, from his post atop the hill, Averell says, he heard the screams of the wounded who had fallen on the slopes in the day's fighting and had not yet been removed, but the situation's full horror did not reveal itself until dawn. Looking down the hill at first light, Averell saw that "[d]ead and wounded men were on the ground in every attitude of distress. A third of them were dead, but enough were alive and moving to give to the field a singular crawling effect" (72).

Averell clearly witnessed much the same sight as Bierce presents in "Chickamauga," but there are also obvious differences between this simple report and Bierce's vivid account. Such differences bring me to the real issue of my study: what "realism" actually consists of in De Forest's and Bierce's Civil War writings. As most authors and critics are quick to point out, simple accuracy of observation, which is all I have concerned myself with thus far, does not constitute realism as a literary style or aesthetic. Realism lies not in just getting the surface appearance right, but in imparting to it some kind of meaning or feeling, in the way that Bierce's grisly details evoke an immediacy of horror and alienation while Averell's bare description and inexpressive adjective "singular" do not. As Howells asserted early on, "When realism becomes false to itself, when it heaps up facts merely, and maps life instead of picturing it, realism will perish" ("Study" 973). Or, as Jackson K. Putnam has stated the case more recently,

> The words "fact" and "truth" do not mean the same thing. The former in ordinary usage refers to something real or existent. . . . The latter term usually carries a "higher" meaning—a scientific conclusion of universal validity based upon reasoning from individual facts, or a literary assertion about the human condition also considered universal and also derived from the facts of human existence. . . . Creative writers imaginatively infuse the term ["truth"] with moral and emotional significance and critics mainly judge the aesthetic success of a literary work according to its capability of yielding this kind of truth. No mere reporting of facts, however accurately done, can make a novel . . . succeed as a work of art, and a story that is confined solely to such reporting is devoid of aesthetic truth and of literary significance. (17)

Putnam's higher meaning, what Howells calls "picturing" and what Crane has Vernall call "an expression of life," means that, Putnam's references to universality notwithstanding, at this point realism inevitably becomes at least partially relative, since no two writers dramatizing the same events will affix the same meaning to them. As Robert Spiller points out with reference to Henry James, realism consists of the author's representing life as it appears *to him*, "which may not be the same as life as it 'really' is" (134). In a similar vein, Harry Levin, struggling with the concept of reality in fiction, finally refuses to define it, "since it cannot bear precisely the same significance for any two human beings" ("Realism" 193). Even De Forest, a most articulate proponent of realism, harbored no illusions about providing anything other than a carefully observed but finally limited and thus subjective impression of life, as he says in commenting to Howells that realism is finally no more "true" than romanticism. These two kinds of fiction, De Forest writes, "are equally allowable and in a certain sense equally true. Each is the result of a selection, for we cannot tell the whole life, even of a country village; we must choose some characters for our painting, and shut our eyes to others. . . . Let each one select what he can best paint" (qtd. in Light 167).

Both De Forest and Bierce understood these limitations of selection, for if they agree on battle's objectively observable aspects and the soldier's immediate response to them, they differ widely on what battle finally means to the soldier and its ultimate effects on him. With this divergence in mind, I will examine these veteran-authors' writings in terms of two related but different kinds of realism, which, following Putnam's terminology, I call "fact" and "truth." Fact comprises those elements I have discussed already: the authors' presentation of the soldier's objectively verifiable actions, thoughts, and feelings in combat. Truth consists of the ways each author uses in his fiction various components—such as setting, action, character, point of view, the details selected for inclusion, and, perhaps most important, style—to create from battle's commonly noted aspects his personal impression of conflict and its consequences for the participant.

Such a study logically begins with the authors' intentions, so far as I can determine them, for these are crucial to the works' final emphases upon fact and truth. Because both De Forest and Bierce aspired to produce serious, artful literature—that is, works containing a higher truth—the simple transcription of their own actual experiences in homely language, in the manner of the Civil War veterans' narratives that proliferated from the 1880s to the end of the century, was not sufficient to their purposes; for reasons that I will explain more fully in the next chapter, such an approach would yield many facts but little truth. Both men, therefore, engaged with models of "literary" writing about battle to develop forms for conveying what they wished to say in both their factual memoirs and their fictions on this subject. The danger in this practice was that the writer ran the risk of sacrificing both the objective accuracy and the intense subjective feeling that his own experience might afford him in favor of the "literary" values of the old rhetoric of the battle-piece. As Levin has observed on this subject, "War is the test case for realistic fiction. No other subject can be so obscured by the ivy of tradition, the crystallization of legend, the conventions of epic and romance" (*Gates* 137). Addressing himself more specifically to Civil War writing, Harold Frederic, in a favorable review of Crane's *Red Badge of Courage,* acutely asserts that what sets this novel apart from most war literature is the immediacy of its vision, its lack of mediation by literary models. In more conventional combat writing, he says, "at best [the author] gives us a conventional account of what happened, but on analysis you find that this is not what he really saw but what all his reading has taught him he must have seen" (32).[1] What I will examine in this study's ensuing chapters is De Forest's and Bierce's handling of this potential pitfall: how successfully each author blends his literary intent and influences with his personal experience in his attempt to create a factually accurate and truthfully persuasive vision of life under fire.

Part II

John W. De Forest

Chapter 4

The Limits of Experience

Both chronologically and critically John W. De Forest is the logical figure with which to begin a study of realism in Civil War battle writing. In nonfiction and fiction alike De Forest was among the earliest published of Civil War authors, contributing articles about his combat experiences to *Harper's New Monthly Magazine* beginning in 1864, while he was still in the field, and releasing his Civil War novel, *Miss Ravenel's Conversion from Secession to Loyalty,* in 1867. More significantly, these works depict the actualities of war in ways that the contemporaneous writings of other authors, such as James Roberts Gilmore's *Among the Pines* (1862), William T. Adams's *Soldier Boy* (1863), Horatio Alger's *Frank's Campaign* (1864), John Townsend Trowbridge's *Three Scouts* (1865), John Esten Cooke's *Surry of Eagle's-Nest* (1866), and Lydia Child's *Romance of the Republic* (1867), do not approach—or, in many cases, even attempt. As Albert E. Stone Jr. notes of *Miss Ravenel's Conversion,* De Forest's "resolute honesty . . . [which] is most clearly manifest in his battlefield and hospital scenes," makes "the bloody episodes in the novels of his more popular contemporaries ring about as true as the libretto of an operetta" (86). Although many critics from De Forest's own day to the present have found this novel flawed in other respects, particularly in the romantic-melodramatic love triangle at its center—comprising Lillie Ravenel, the novel's eponymous high-spirited Southern heroine, Colonel Carter, the brave and dashing but morally weak Union officer who marries her and then betrays her with the more seductive Mrs. Larue, and Captain Colburne, the noble subordinate of Carter's who loves Lillie from afar and wins her after the colonel's death in battle—none denies De Forest's achievement in his combat scenes.[1]

Perhaps an even more important reason to treat De Forest first is that, in addition to pioneering the publication of realistic war fiction and nonfiction alike, he was also an insightful critic of these genres. In a number of essays and reviews for the *Atlantic Monthly,* he produced a body of critical writings that offer a more fully articulated theory about what constitutes realism in combat literature than any other author of his era. Beginning with this theory will provide a benchmark for his own practice in his other work and for Bierce's work as well.

De Forest's most systematic analysis of battle writing appears, as noted earlier, in his 1879 *Atlantic Monthly* article "Our Military Past and Future," in which he seeks to persuade his readers that military reforms are necessary to prepare the United States for its next war. Among the most crucial of these reforms, in De Forest's view, is the development of a more thorough program of military instruction than that which America has hitherto accorded its armed forces. Under the army's current slipshod training methods, De Forest asserts, soldiers commonly arrive on the battlefield with little idea of what will happen to them in this environment and consequently make a very poor showing. He contends that training that acquaints recruits as thoroughly as possible with the actualities of combat will improve their performance under fire,[2] and since his idea of preparation entails more reading than drilling, it is on this issue that literary criticism takes its place in this article. As one of his proposals, De Forest calls for requiring the young men who constitute the nation's military reserve to study military science at their public schools and universities. He outlines a reading course that would begin with textbooks on strategic and tactical theories but would move quickly beyond such abstractions to the study of battle history, for he believes that reading accounts of previous battles is the best way for the prospective soldier to prepare for coming under fire. Not just any history will do, however; to be useful to the student, the accounts must be realistic.

De Forest begins his definition of realism in this context with the attack quoted near the beginning of this study on the "host of ignorant romancers calling themselves historians." The student seeking enlightenment about combat does not need this group's "trashy, misleading" accounts, "which prattle of 'billows of cavalry' and 'infantry standing like rocks,'" but rather "books which show just what war is, and what to do amidst its perplexities and difficulties" (572). "Just what war is" for De Forest becomes clear in the ensuing paragraphs, and his description closely matches the historians' and psychologists' reports discussed in the preceding chapter.[3] He is first at pains to dispel misconceptions on the large tactical level, with eyewitness reports that corroborate Gerald F. Linderman's explanations of Civil War combat methods. De Forest says, "There are no more billows of cavalry, if there ever were any; cavalry dismounts now, and fires from behind walls and thickets and other cover; only now and then does it steal a charge on other cavalry, or on broken infantry,—never on infantry not already broken. Nor does infantry stand like a rock, but rather like reeds shaken by the wind" (572).

The last image in this passage, with its indication of individual rather than group responses, brings De Forest to his second and preeminent point, which is the same central truth about combat that Ardant du Picq, S. L. A. Marshall, and John Keegan emphasize. A military unit under fire is not an imperturbable monolith under its officers' absolute control, but rather a collection of individuals constantly beset by fear and thus constantly on the verge of responding as undisciplined individuals to their separate impulses to either fire or flee, at best held together provisionally by their officers and their own loyalty to one another. "A military history is useless, or even noxious," De Forest asserts, "which does not clearly show that even the best soldiers sometimes reel under blasts of destruction." Infantry in combat, he explains, stands as well as it can against shrieking flights of missiles, scattering wounds and death. It stands firmest when it lies down, using what shelter and hiding it can find,—a ripple of ground, clumps of bushes, tall herbage. It stands, not in solid masses, but in fragile groups or slender lines, swaying backwards and forwards unexpectedly, gaping open here and there with slaughter or sudden quailing, cobbled into temporary form by hoarse and anxious officers, supported hastily by panting reinforcements, doing its suffering best perhaps, but not at all like a rock. (572)

Like the soldiers' behavior, the sights of battle only slightly resemble the ignorant romancers' accounts of them. In a description similar to Richard Holmes's discussion of the battlefield's appearance, De Forest says that, word-paintings of billows and rocks notwithstanding,

[t]he columns of attack which one reads of are [in reality] frail and fluctuating threads, for the most part dragging wearily along as if on a march, though sometimes breaking forth in brief, partial spurts. What they advance against the spectator can seldom discern with the eye; he only guesses it when a long, light roll of smoke leaps from the earth in front, followed by a continuous harsh roar; something invisible and perhaps altogether unexpected is causing regiments and brigades to vanish away. Or if the charge succeeds, it seems marvelous that the defeated should have fled, the conquerors look so scattered and so few. (572)

Inaccuracies regarding behavior and sight are not simply problematic in themselves, De Forest continues, for when a writer devotes himself to turns of vivid rhetoric he creates a larger difficulty: a lack of cause and effect. To educate a student of military science, an account of a battle must not only contain facts—truthfully documenting how soldiers behave under fire and the way battle looks—but also demonstrate the reasons that one army won and the other lost; in historical terms, this is the higher truth the serious writer should attempt to develop. However,

[a]s history is usually written, an ordinary civilian may read about

campaigns and battles all his life, without ever really knowing why one army failed and another succeeded. His first supposition probably is that the victors were braver than the vanquished. Then he is puzzled to account for the apparently resulting fact that Germans, for instance, are sometimes braver than Frenchmen, and sometimes not so brave. If he is a liberal in politics, he explains this by talking about "the spirit of an age." If he is a hero-worshiper, he speaks of the genius of Frederick, or the genius of Napoleon. But in neither case can he show the process by which his favorite cause produced the given effect. (573)

De Forest's basic criteria for good military writing are thus quite simple: it must accurately depict the actions and sights of combat, and it must explain why a battle unfolded as it did. From the outset De Forest meets these criteria in his own military writing, as an examination of his first effort in this area will demonstrate. This initial piece, an article on his own introduction to combat entitled "The First Time Under Fire," which was first published in the *Harper's Monthly* issue of September 1864 and then included, in revised form, as the fourth chapter of his book devoted to his wartime experiences, *A Volunteer's Adventures*,[4] reveals an unswerving concern with accuracy and clarity. De Forest begins this account on an emphatically unromantic note, saying that although the members of his regiment, the Twelfth Connecticut, have marched triumphantly as conquerors into New Orleans after Admiral Farragut's naval victory forced the city's Confederate defenders to retire, they have not yet come under fire. All they know of war is what any occupation force in a humid Southern climate quickly learns: "what it [is] to suffer; to wilt under a Southern sun, and be daubed with Louisiana mud; to be sick by hundreds and die by scores" (475).[5] These afflictions seem less onerous when the regiment receives word that it may soon go into action as part of an expeditionary force into the Louisiana interior, but De Forest sacrifices any excitement he might here stir in a reader for an explanation of the true method of setting out for battle. Marching off to fight, the Twelfth Connecticut do not simply seize their muskets with a lusty hurrah and follow their general into the jaws of hell. Rather, their general, Godfrey Weitzel, initially doubts the Twelfth's combat readiness, having heard rumors that the regiment is "not only sickly but broken in spirit and undisciplined" (475). To earn its place in Weitzel's force, the regiment must demonstrate its efficiency in a lengthy close-order drill under the general's personal command. Thus, the real key to success in battle, as De Forest points out in "Our Military Past and Future," is not pure heroism but a focus on the mundane details of preparation. The Twelfth marches out with Weitzel, in De Forest's antiromantic simile, because in drill "we went like a watch" (475).

Having established his own regiment's part in this expedition, De Forest then shifts to a wider angle of vision so that the reader will grasp the cause-and-effect pattern of the ensuing battle of Labadieville, which, he notes, "was the most scientific combat, or at least the very luckiest one in regard to combinations effecting their logical results, that I ever witnessed" (477). The "combinations" that De Forest refers to are Weitzel's strategic precautions and troop dispositions. Marching his force up both sides of a bayou, Weitzel keeps the majority of his troops on the left bank, De Forest explains, because it is wider and therefore affords a better line of possible retreat. Weitzel also orders a detachment of his troops to be ready at notice to cut down the high embankments of the levees that border the bayou, thereby enabling him to use a pontoon bridge to move reinforcements, if necessary, rapidly from one side of the bayou to the other. These preparations quickly pay off when they conjoin with some of the good luck that De Forest has been careful to credit as having a share in any victory. Weitzel's scouts on the right bank spot a Confederate ambush awaiting the column, and what follows is "an illustration of two great military principles, the value of time and the value of concentration" (477). In simple, straightforward language and with careful attention to logical structure—first describing troops' placements and then detailing the reasons for those placements—De Forest provides an overview of the field to explain the causal roles time and concentration play in the ensuing events:

> To exhibit [these roles] I must state the enemy's position, forces, and intentions. I have already observed that his right wing, posted on the left bank of the bayou [the left from De Forest's point of view], and consisting of a regiment of infantry and a battery of six field-pieces, was held well back, or, in military parlance, refused, being probably meant to merely amuse our main column. His centre, on the right

bank, was composed of four field-pieces, a regiment of [local] militia and two regiments of veterans.... His left wing, five hundred cavalry and two field-pieces, was at this moment making a large circuit by a country road, with the idea of coming upon the rear [of the Union right].... [Confederate commander] Mouton's plan was an excellent one. He did not mean that his weak right wing should fight seriously, unless it should be necessary to keep his centre from being flanked or turned. His veterans were to repulse [the Union right], and his cavalry was to cut off its escape. There was only one flaw; he knew nothing of the pontoon bridge. The whole question was whether Weitzel could concentrate his main force against Mouton's centre and break it before the cavalry of the latter could get into action on our rear. (477)

With the battle's overall shape clearly outlined so that the reader can see the centrality of time and concentration, De Forest returns to a narrower view, explaining what he and the men of his regiment do and see as Mouton's and Weitzel's maneuvers play themselves out. The Twelfth Connecticut is part of the Union main force on the left bank, and it is ordered to cross the pontoon bridge and join Weitzel's concentration against the Confederate center on the right bank. At this stage, De Forest has no idea of the larger tactical picture of which his men are a part; all he knows is that he must get his company across the bridge and into the assault as quickly as possible, and his insights about himself and his men as he does so closely parallel John Dollard's and others' findings about men's feelings and behavior in combat. Over and over De Forest indicates that he fails to notice any fear in himself because, like Dollard's veterans, he is too busy concentrating on the job immediately at hand. At the bridge he sees his first wounded man and comes under fire for the first time, but his reactions to these things focus on his responsibilities, not on apprehension for himself. He describes the wounded man in unflinching detail—"his knee crushed by a shot, his torn trowsers soaked with a dirty crimson, his face a ghastly yellow, and his eyes looking the agony of death" (477)—but reports that his only concern is with his company's morale. "I did not want my men to see this dismaying spectacle," he explains, "and called their attention to something, I have forgotten what, which was passing on the other side of the bayou" (477). When, a moment later, De Forest steps onto the pontoon bridge and artillery shells begin bursting close to him, again he finds his concerns limited to the immediately practical: "I remember that my chief anxiety while crossing was lest I should wet my feet in the sloppy bottom of the flat-boat" (477).

These reactions elicit from De Forest an assessment of his feelings that anticipates later combat psychologists' insights about the various phases of fear on the battlefield. A veteran, De Forest says—and as Dollard and S. L. A. Marshall confirm eighty years later—can tell when he is in imminent danger and when he is not, and he knows enough to be afraid when he is. But as a novice, De Forest does not possess this discernment; concern with his task and simple ignorance keep him from feeling any fear at all. "[O]n the present occasion," he says,

> I was not oppressed by any feeling which could be called even alarm. I was buoyed up by the physical excitement of rapid movement, by my anxiety that my company should do well, and by my ignorance of the profounder, the really tremendous horrors into which battle may develop. . . . I had no nervous inclination to duck, no involuntary twitching or trembling; I was not aware of any painful quickening of the pulse; in short, I was not frightened. I thought to myself, It is very possible that they will hit me, but I hope not, and I think not. It seemed to me the most natural thing in the world that others should be killed, and that I should not. I have suffered more in every engagement since than I did in this first trial. It is a frequent, it is the usual experience. (478–79)

At this point De Forest is also ignorant of the way men behave in battle and what the battlefield looks like; the rest of the article documents his learning process in these areas. Once across the pontoon bridge, De Forest's regiment advances in close order until it reaches the impediments of two rail fences and some large thorn thickets. Far from acting as one, the regiment passes these obstacles disjointedly, its formation dissolving as some men push the fence down in spots and others climb over it and all become entangled in the thickets' briers. De Forest the veteran, writing the article, knows that "[t]he best-disciplined troops will not come up to the scratch in good order when it is a case of charging brambles and briers" (478).

However, De Forest the greenhorn company commander still has notions of infantry "standing like rocks." He and the regiment's other company officers desperately shout orders for their struggling men to close up, because "[i]n our inexperience we believed that all was lost if the regiment did not march shoulder to shoulder as if it were on review; and from here onward, all the way through the battle, we labored for a straight line" (478).

De Forest's inexperience leads to further surprises a moment later, when the Twelfth reaches an open field and comes under enemy musket fire for the first time; neither the battlefield itself nor his reactions to it are what De Forest expects them to be. The first evidence of the enemy's near presence, he reports, using a simile calculated to be familiar to the average reader, is "a long rattle like that which a boy makes in running with a stick along a picket fence, only vastly louder." Then he hears the "sharp, quick *whit whit*" of Confederate bullets, but all he can see of the men attempting to kill him is "a long, low blue roll of smoke" (479). As the regiment advances over the field toward the Confederates entrenched beneath this smoke, De Forest sees bullets actually accomplishing their purpose, including a particularly horrible wound quite near him: "On the right of me a sharp crash, as of bones broken by a hatchet, drew my attention, and looking that way, I saw Edwards, one of the color-bearers, fall slowly backwards, raising one hand to his mouth as the blood spirted [*sic*] from it; an 'Oh!' of pain or alarm burst from his lips, and in his eyes there was a stare of woeful amazement" (479).

However, De Forest reacts differently to this spectacle than he thought he might. "I had expected," he notes, "that such sights as this would be depressing and terrible. It was not so; it was not even painful; it hardly seemed unnatural; it only produced a feeling of surprise" (479). He is additionally surprised that his muted reaction is the common one, as he realizes when he watches another of his men pick up the colors from the wounded man's hand and march on, "calmly chewing his tobacco" (479).

With the stage thus set for an advance under fire, the moment is right for an ignorant romancer to unfurl a "clarion-like narrative . . . that . . . leads on the victors to easy triumph," as De Forest describes battle-pieces in another article ("Recent Literature" 406). De Forest, however, is less concerned with rhetorical splendor than with demonstrating an assault's actual nature—its stops and starts, its confusions, its disjointedness, its dependence as much on good luck as on good management. The attack begins fitfully, De Forest reports, because while some officers order their men to advance, others order theirs to lie down; this confusion resolves itself only when the regiment's colonel succeeds in making his order for the entire force to move forward heard over the musketry. Then, rather than advancing in open order, which would enable them to move quickly and make them difficult targets, the men bunch together toward the colors in the center, instinctively seeking the comfort of close contact in the face of danger but in doing so impeding one another's movements and creating an easy mass for the enemy to shoot at. Working determinedly, De Forest and the other officers manage to spread their line, only to discover a new threat when they see that the officers of the regiment supporting them on their left have not been so successful and that this regiment is falling back in disorder, the working of its "delicate tactical machinery" (480) hopelessly broken.

Nevertheless, the men of the Twelfth advance, firing as they go, although they have little idea of what they are firing at; De Forest notes that many in the regiment never see the enemy throughout the battle. He himself does not catch sight of any Confederates until he has traversed more than half the field, and what he sees is again not what he expects. Braced for a line of gray-clad men grimly determined to hold their positions with bayonets, "not knowing then that hand-to-hand combats exist mainly in newspapers" (480), De Forest instead sees "a crowd of men spring up from behind the fence in front of us, plunge across the road, and sweep into the forest, seeming to be actually jumping over one another in their haste, and looking, in their gray uniforms, like an immense flock of sheep swarming over a fence" (480).

With the Confederates in retreat, an accident completes the Twelfth's victory. Another Union regiment appears on the Twelfth's left, and, excited by the sight of the fleeing Confederates, its members ignore their colonel's order not to fire and add their volley to the Twelfth's. This unexpected support further emboldens the men of the Twelfth, who exultantly carry the Confederates' fence and then continue to fire into the forest even after the enemy has completely vanished. De Forest immediately attempts to get his men to cease fire, explaining that, in his inexperience regarding what winning an engagement feels like, "I was in a state of amazement at what seemed to me the feeble resistance of the enemy, and was far from supposing that we had broken his main force and won the battle" (480). He believes that the Twelfth has simply driven off a party of skirmishers. Only when Weitzel himself rides up to congratulate the regiment does De Forest realize the battle is over.

The reader familiar with conventional battle writing might expect here a full-blown inspirational address from the general, full of references to the men's strength of arms and the rightness of their cause, such as the one British historian Sir Edward Creasy reports as having been delivered before the Greek victory over the Persians at Marathon in 490 B.C. In his highly popular and influential *Fifteen Decisive Battles of the World,* first published in 1851, Creasy says that "along the mountain slopes of Marathon must have resounded the mutual exhortation, which . . . was afterward heard over the waves of Salamis: 'On, sons of the Greeks! Strike for the freedom of your country! Strike for the freedom of your children and of your wives—for the shrines of your fathers' gods, and for the sepulchres of your sires. All—all are now staked upon the strife'" (35).[6]

De Forest, however, once again tacitly deconstructs the battle-piece, depicting Weitzel as being as wholly concerned with practicalities as Dollard's veterans are—or as De Forest reports himself to have been during the engagement. "'Twelfth Connecticut,'" De Forest quotes the general, "'you have done well. That is the way to do it. Never stop, and the enemy won't stop'" (481). The regiment's response to this "very compendium of practical instruction," as De Forest admiringly terms it, is three cheers, with this approval of practicality over bombast seeming to confirm their maturation in combat.[7]

With his own and his regiment's part in the battle completed, De Forest returns to the larger issues of cause and effect in the conflict's outcome. The destruction of the Confederate center, in which the Twelfth played its role, frustrates the Confederate left wing's movement around the Union right to attempt an attack from the rear, for this left wing has to retreat to avoid being cut off from the Confederate main body. His flanking strategy defeated and his entire army threatened, Confederate General Mouton has no choice but to retreat. De Forest here reiterates the principal reasons for this result, tying up the points he made in his introductory tactical overview: "Weitzel won his . . . victory by dint of concentration and of promptness of movement; and the possibility of these flowed from the forethought which provided his rude but serviceable pontoon-bridge" (482).

The civilian reader can thus see from the theoretical viewpoint why the Federals won and the Confederates lost—Weitzel executed his tactical conception more effectively than Mouton did—but this explanation does not answer the related question of *why* Weitzel was able to do so, why Weitzel's men performed better in attacking the Confederate center than Mouton's did in defending it. The reader confronted with conventional battle writing would have no choice, as De Forest notes in "Our Military Past and Future," but to fall back on notions of the Union army's being braver than the Confederate, or Weitzel's being a better general than Mouton, or the spirit of the age favoring the Union. De Forest is careful, however, to point out a more specific cause, a combination of tactics and psychology:

> I think the success of our regiment in charging veterans in a strong position was owing very much to the file-fire which we kept up while advancing. In the first place, it supported the spirits of our men, who believed that they were doing as much damage as they received, and felt that they ought to be able to bear the trial as long as the enemy. In the second place, it killed the musketry of the rebels, who, unfortunately for their morale, I think, had for shelter a deep plantation ditch, which served them for the purpose of a rifle-pit. Now a human being who has a cover in battle hates to put his head outside of it. As a proof that we actually did overwhelm and derange the hostile musketry, I may adduce the fact that we had only six men hit by bullets. The rebels lost very few, to be sure; but the fence above their heads was so tattered by our shot as to be a curiosity; and the prisoners said that, what with the whizzing of Miniés and the flying of cypress splinters, the ditch was a most unpleasant position. (482)

De Forest then concludes the article by moving from such tactical explanations to the larger strategic picture, explaining this particular battle's place in Weitzel's overall campaign. Weitzel planned at the expedition's outset to defeat the Confederates in a pitched battle and then push the left and right wings of his army out ahead of the retreating enemy to cut off their escape. This plan fails, De Forest says, because the victory he has just described is actually too complete; rather than retreating slowly and thus giving the Union flanks time to encircle them, the Confederates have been so badly beaten and so intimidated that they flee precipitately and thereby escape Weitzel's trap.

At the conclusion the reader has seen clearly and at length what men witness and how they behave under fire, and how that behavior, coupled with various other factors, creates the outcomes of battles and campaigns. Plainly, De Forest's nonfiction battle writing meets his own criteria for realism as he expresses them in "Our Military Past and Future."

De Forest also applies these standards to his war fiction. Toward the end of *Miss Ravenel's Conversion* Lillie and her father, Dr. Ravenel, receive a letter from Captain Colburne describing the recent Union victory at Cedar Creek, Virginia, at which Colburne was present. After listening to his daughter read this narrative, the doctor praises it in terms that closely echo De Forest's words in "Our Military Past and Future": "Really, that is a most brilliant letter.... That is the most splendid battle-piece that ever was produced by any author, ancient or modern.... Neither Tacitus nor Napier can equal it. Alison is all fudge and claptrap with his granite squares of infantry and his billows of cavalry. One can understand Colburne. I know just how that battle of Cedar Creek was fought, and I almost think that I could fight such an [*sic*] one myself. There is cause and effect and their relations to each other in his narrative" (439).

It is significant that De Forest has Dr. Ravenel praise the writing of a soldier who was an eyewitness to the events he relates. The reason so many military histories fall short of realism's requirements, De Forest says in "Our Military Past and Future," is that most are the work of civilians who lack the firsthand battle experience that would show them the errors of their "rhetorical generalities" (572). He takes this matter up in more detail and more pointedly in an *Atlantic Monthly* review of historian James A. Froude's biography of Julius Caesar. Terming the book "fairly reliable" on the whole, De Forest notes "one extremely regrettable imperfection": "Here is the life of a great soldier written by a man who knows nothing of soldierly matters.... The consequence is that the account of military transactions teems with misconceptions, which are rather brought to light than hidden by vivid phrases and impetuous narrative.... [O]ne is reminded of the battle-pieces of the eloquent reporters of our civil war, who gathered their impossible particulars afar from the scene of conflict, and who 'did not know a manoeuvre from a hole in the ground'" ("Recent Literature" 406).

Given this emphasis on firsthand observation and practical experience, one might readily conclude that De Forest's own accounts of Civil War battles ought to be effectively realistic by his own definition—revealing "just what war is" in terms of sight, action, and cause and effect—simply because De Forest himself met the preconditions of observation and experience. As he recounts in his introduction to his volume of poems, *Medley and Palestina,* he served forty-six days under fire: six days of pitched battle, three days with storming parties, and thirty-seven days of siege (ix); and in an 1898 interview with *New York Times* reporter Edwin Oviatt, De Forest remarks that, although he had written two novels prior to this one—*Witching Times* in 1856–57 and *Seacliff; or The Mystery of the Westerveldts* in 1859, it was only in *Miss Ravenel's Conversion* that "'for the first time in my life I came to know the value of personal knowledge of one's subject and the art of drawing upon life. . . . From my *Miss Ravenel* on I have written from life and been a realist'" (40–41). And indeed, at least one critic has taken De Forest at his literal word on this point. Stanley T. Williams, in his introduction to *A Volunteer's Adventures,* cites its "unadorned reality" and asserts that "[i]n writing the passages on battle in *Miss Ravenel's Conversion* [De Forest] merely remembered his daily life" as he recorded it in this volume (vii).

Certainly this statement is true in the narrowest sense: *A Volunteer's Adventures* is De Forest's recollection of his daily military life, and many of the incidents in it reappear only slightly altered in *Miss Ravenel's Conversion.* As Williams of course knows, however, more is involved in writing about battle, as about any subject, than simply transcribing one's memories as they come to mind. Memory itself is notoriously unhelpful when a veteran sets out to describe the experience of combat, chiefly because that experience is so stressful that often the participant's recollections of it fade almost immediately. Battle for many soldiers is, in Richard Holmes's phrase, "a half-remembered blur, a mosaic somehow fragmented and haphazardly reassembled" (263). Similarly, novelist and Vietnam veteran Tim O'Brien says that "[i]n any war story, but especially a true one, it's difficult to separate what happened from what seemed to happen. . . . The angles of vision are skewed. . . . The pictures get jumbled; you tend to miss a lot. And then afterward, when you go to tell about it, there is always that surreal seemingness, which makes the story seem untrue, but which in fact represents the hard and exact truth as it *seemed*" (78).

Many Civil War combatants attested to this phenomenon, which they discerned even while they were still in the field. Writing in May 1864, Oliver Wendell Holmes Jr. notes that the sharp edges of combat reality "rapidly escape the memory in the mist which settles over a fought field"; on 4 July of that same year, Union volunteer Daniel Crotty sums up his three years of service with the remark that "now that we have passed through such bloody ordeals, we cannot realize fully that we have experienced such tiresome marches and fearful battles. As we look over the past, to most of us it seems like a dream" (both qtd. in Linderman 267).

Even when the writer does retain a sharp recollection of combat, as Holmes says some soldiers do and as De Forest evidently did, if we judge by the consistent specificity of *A Volunteer's Adventures,* relying solely on one's own memory poses risks. In his essay "The Great American Novel" De Forest asserts that such a novel is "a tale which paints American life so broadly, truly, and sympathetically that every American of feeling and culture is forced to acknowledge the picture as a likeness of something which he knows" (28). If a similar universality of recognition is the battle writer's goal, his own experiences, however accurately recalled, will be inadequate to his purpose, for, as Holmes points out, the writer thereby "risks discovering a universality where none might exist" (9). British historian Basil Liddell Hart states the problem more fully in *Strategy: The Indirect Approach:* "Direct experience is inherently too limited to form an adequate foundation either for theory or for application [regarding combat]. At best it produces an atmosphere that is of value in drying and hardening the structure of thought. The great value of indirect experience lies in its greater variety and extent" (23–24).

Moreover, if the writer intends to reproduce not only the battle's sights and actions but also its cause-and-effect pattern, he likewise requires more information than his personal recollections can supply, particularly if, as De Forest did, he spent most of his service in the ranks. As I noted in my first chapter, soldiers at this level in the Civil War had no way of attaining on their own a large-scale tactical and strategic grasp of the events in which they participated. In this wide sense, S. L. A. Marshall points out,

> [b]attle is a fog for the men who fight. The small unit will usually remain in the dark about its own achievement unless someone from higher up clarifies "the big picture." And that is done automatically in but few cases.... Thus it happens that a company or battalion may win a victory under circumstances which make it appear almost as a defeat on the local ground, either because it is overconscious of its own hard losses or because the over-all tactical effect could be seen only at the higher headquarters. (121–22)

These requirements for some of the raw materials on which he will work are reason enough in themselves for the battle writer to turn to sources beyond his own memories, but he may also be impelled toward such sources by deeper needs. As is the case with any kind of literature, not just combat writing, assembling material is one thing, while selecting the telling details from it, conveying them in language that makes them palpable to a reader, and presenting them in a manner that reveals an underlying meaning is quite another. But these difficulties are especially acute when one deals with combat, since this is an environment marked to an even greater extent than more everyday events by chaos and an apparent lack of cause and effect. Simply finding words that adequately describe one's experiences under fire can be a major stumbling block. One difficulty is the difference between military and civilian language. Like the argot of most professions, much of what soldiers say, especially the terms in which they frame combat, is intelligible only to other soldiers. As sociologist J. A. Blake notes, "The language of combat reality is an exhortatory, private language," the main function of which "is its instrumentality—instigating and furthering action" (334). Beyond this barrier is an even more restrictive one, many soldiers' inability to frame their experiences in any words whatsoever. American combat historian Nat Frankel describes interviewing many World War II veterans "with an actual lust to tell their tales of Armageddon. But once they start, even the most articulate of them fall tongue-tied. What was Iwo Jima like? It was . . . it was . . . it was fucking rough man! I know that, but what was it like? Really . . . really . . . really tough! So the very experience of war, what would seem to be the prerequisite for describing it, precluded any actual, palpable narrative" (19).

Faced with these difficulties of matter and execution, the writer usually prepares himself for his task in the same way that De Forest suggests the soldier should prepare for his, by examining what others before him have done in his situation. A certain irony presents itself here in connection with De Forest's proposals in "Our Military Past and Future." De Forest calls for potential soldiers to read military history, but, as many combat psychologists—including Holmes, Marshall, and Keegan—point out, soldiers learn more about their profession from their own firsthand observations than from studying others' experiences, while battle writers learn more about their craft from reading than from personal experience of their subject. As Keegan states the case, "[I]f soldiers did not learn to fight their battles from reading books, neither is it likely that military historians learnt to write their books from watching battles. Battles are extremely confusing; and confronted with the need to make sense of something he does not understand, even the cleverest, indeed preeminently the cleverest man, realizing his need for a language and metaphor he does not possess, will turn to look at what someone else has already made as a guide for his own pen" (63).

Numerous critics have observed the effects of such a turning to guides in American war writing. Both Kathleen Diffley and Lee Steinmetz note many Civil War writers' recourse to familiar forms to find a language and metaphor that would make the war comprehensible to their audiences. Diffley traces the frequent occurrences of familiarly sexually coded language in popular writers' works on the war, in which the masculine North subdues the feminine South (364); Steinmetz says that one of the most popular contemporary forms of Civil War literature, the extended narrative in verse, almost invariably used a single formula drawn from melodrama—the noble hero's separation from his pure lady-love through the machinations of an utterly black-hearted villain (175–77). These facts, in Diffley's words, "demonstrate . . . how the sentimental ideal provided both terms and a pattern for [popular writers'] use in organizing events" (364).

David Lundberg and David Kennedy trace a similar search for terms and patterns by World War I writers, with similarly sentimental results. Lundberg points out that for some American writers—Hemingway, Dos Passos, E. E. Cummings—as for their European counterparts, "[s]o overwhelming was the slaughter that . . . it could not be described in conventional terms. New forms of writing were needed. Indeed, a new literary consciousness was required" (377). But for most American veterans, who saw relatively little combat and thus did not share the Europeans' sense of disillusionment, the search for forms in which to convey their experiences led not to invention but to a falling back on the familiar, on the platitudes with which the United States government had sent them off to France in the first place. Kennedy notes that "[n]ot only did many doughboys accept without reflection the official definitions of the war's meaning, but perhaps more important, they translated that meaning into their understanding of their personal experiences, and described those experiences in language transported directly from the pious and inflated pronouncements of the spokesmen for traditional culture. That language pervades all the vast 'literature' produced during the war by members of the AEF" (213).

De Forest firmly believed in personal experience, in writing from life without mediation by narrative formulas or received platitudes, as the foundation of realism, as his comments to Oviatt demonstrate. In this vein, he has the narrator in his second novel, *Seacliff,* assert that "[f]rom the moment [the writer] depends for inspiration on other literary works, instead of the truth about people, he is doomed to fail as an artist" (270). Nevertheless, when he joined the Union army in 1862 as the captain of Company I of the Twelfth Connecticut Volunteers, he was, at thirty-five, an established writer of ten years' standing, with five books to his credit, all of which were informed by his own avid reading of and theorizing about writers he believed had themselves caught "the truth about people"; and it is clear that he brought this background to *Miss Ravenel's Conversion* as well. Eric Solomon notes that the novel's combination of war and romance plots, with the war advancing the romance, is derived from Walter Scott and James Fenimore Cooper, and that the romantic triangle of innocent Lillie, philandering Carter, and devoted Colburne is heavily indebted to Thackeray's *Vanity Fair* ("Novelist" 82–83). Gordon Haight points out the influence of not only Thackeray and Scott but also Dickens and George Eliot (vi), while Edmund Wilson adds Stendhal to this list (684) and Daniel Aaron mentions Balzac ("Civil War" 172). Given this wide use of literary models and the copious knowledge of military history that De Forest's review essays demonstrate, it is logical to inquire whether De Forest likewise drew on what he considered the best battle writing to give form to his own combat narratives. And a natural corollary to this question is a second question: if he used sources besides personal experience, did he avoid the pitfall, as Harold Frederic describes it, of writing "not what he really saw but what all his reading has taught him he must have seen"? The answer to both questions is yes, as the next chapter will demonstrate.

CHAPTER 5

The Uses of Influence

Heretofore, critics have not sought out the writers of military history upon whom De Forest may have drawn in his handling of battle scenes, restricting themselves instead to the influence of other fiction writers on his work in this area. Regarding such scenes in *Miss Ravenel's Conversion,* Daniel Aaron (*Unwritten War* 172), Edmund Wilson (684), and Gordon Haight (v) point to Stendhal's *Charterhouse of Parma* and its picture of the battle of Waterloo as the primary source. Insofar as Stendhal's account is "totally nonheroic" (Wilson 684), focusing not on the glory of the charge but rather on the emptiness of the battlefield, the horror of wounds and death, the common soldier's lack of understanding of his circumstances, and the collapse of an army's discipline in defeat, they are correct. Stendhal, however, affords no model for a detailed, coherent explanation of an engagement or part of an engagement from beginning to end, which is as much De Forest's goal in his fiction as in his nonfiction.

Stendhal concerns himself solely with the fragmented experience of his protagonist, Fabrizio Valserra, on the fringes of the battlefield; he never depicts actual combat, only the impressions of one who skirts the field, occasionally coming under long-range cannon fire and participating in the defeated army's retreat.

Aaron and Haight cite De Forest's admiration for Thackeray not only as a chronicler of romance but also as a battle writer, but in fact the case is much the same as with Stendhal. Like De Forest, Thackeray takes a decidedly nonheroic approach to battle. In both *Vanity Fair* and *Henry Esmond* he emphasizes its cost in human life rather than its glory, and in *Henry Esmond* he pointedly takes historians to task for "describing the valour of heroes and the grandeur of conquest" while ignoring "scenes, so brutal, mean, and degrading, that yet form by far the greater part of the drama of war" (277). Like Stendhal, however, Thackeray actually describes battles only briefly and generally, with none of the attention to the hows and whys of their outcome that De Forest sees as necessary to a truly realistic picture of war. For *attitudes* toward war that influenced De Forest, then, we may look to Stendhal and Thackeray, but for models of how actually to *depict* combat realistically we must look beyond them.

Fortunately, De Forest himself simplifies the task of tracing such influences, for in several places he names the military authors he admires. Given his emphasis on a combination of knowledge of military science and firsthand experience as the basis of realistic combat writing, it is not surprising that most of these authors are professional soldiers who wrote about campaigns in which they took part. In "Our Military Past and Future," for example, De Forest lists five writers as having produced "practical and instructive" histories (573), and three fall into this category: Julius Caesar, Napoleon, and, interestingly, in light of Keegan's and Dr. Ravenel's assessments of his work, Sir William Napier. The remaining two are civilians, but one, Alexander Kinglake, could at least claim firsthand knowledge of his subject, for he was present as a correspondent at a number of the battles he recounts in his *Invasion of the Crimea*. The only nonsoldier and noneyewitness to earn De Forest's approval is Thomas Carlyle, for his biography of Frederick the Great.

Despite his admiration for all five of these men, however, De Forest regards one far above the rest. "Caesar's Art of War and of Writing," an essay in the September 1879 *Atlantic Monthly,* is De Forest's homage to this figure; assessing Caesar's *Commentaries,* De Forest declares it "the best military narrative that ever was written" because of its combination of "professional value" in its matter and, in its original Latin, a "perfectly perspicuous and gracefully simple manner" (288). The professional value of the volume, De Forest says, lies chiefly in Caesar's refusal to weight his account with any particular ideological slant. Unlike Tacitus, "who at times appears to be lecturing the Romans on morals instead of furnishing them accurate information, Caesar evidently wants to tell only the actual facts" (286). De Forest also points out that Caesar understands the necessity for clear cause-and-effect delineations, for from among the "actual facts" he makes an "unfailing selection of causative facts" for emphasis and consistently demonstrates "indifference to uninfluential particulars" (288). What makes Caesar's manner of rendering these causative facts so perfectly perspicuous and gracefully simple is his "clear and logical arrangement of matter," his "apparent scorn of mere diction," and his "[e]xtreme simplicity and naturalness" of style. Nothing, De Forest asserts, "could be more high bred, more thoroughly like the speech of a finished gentleman, and less given to points and artifices of rhetoric" (287–88). He finds none of these merits surprising, for in his view the military genius that the *Commentaries* documents makes the book's sterling qualities inevitable, since "[t]he constant composition of orders and instructions teaches a [successful] general to be lucid and short, and leads him to look upon the contrary qualities with distaste. Moreover, the great soldier is by birthright a clear and quick thinker, and his literary utterance is naturally a reflex of his mental operations" (288).

De Forest similarly praises Caesar in his fiction—specifically, in *Miss Ravenel's Conversion.* In the preceding chapter I noted Dr. Ravenel's praise of Colburne's account of the battle of Cedar Creek for its concern with "'cause and effect and their relation to one another'" (439). Earlier in the novel De Forest has Ravenel declare one of Colburne's other letters describing a battle "'equal in precision, brevity, elegance, and every other classical quality of style, to the Commentaries of Julius Caesar'" (207).

With this opinion of Caesar in mind, we might readily ascribe the high quality of both matter and manner in De Forest's own battle writing to the American's modeling his work on the Roman's. As we have seen in "The

First Time Under Fire," De Forest is as careful as he says Caesar is to emphasize cause and effect, to select only the influential particulars, and to make his style and language as straightforward as possible. Therefore, the great degree of realism in his battle writing seems to stem from the combination of experience and reading that De Forest identifies in "Our Military Past and Future" as the source of realism in other combat writers' work, the experience confirming the accuracy of what he has read and the reading providing him with a literary aesthetic by which to present that experience. The answers to the questions that close the preceding chapter thus seem quite simple. De Forest *did* use sources besides his personal experience, and he escaped the danger of allowing such sources to dilute the realism of his own experiences by choosing only such sources as were themselves undilutedly realistic.

This formulation contains a serious difficulty, however: De Forest's evaluation of Caesar as a great combat realist widely misses the mark. As John Keegan points out, Caesar, the primary influence on military writing from the Renaissance to the present, is in fact the father of the battle-piece at its unrevelatory worst.[1] To discover Caesar's failings, let us consider Keegan's analysis of one representative battle account in the *Commentaries,* Caesar's description of his defeat of the Gallic tribe the Nervii on the River Sambre, in modern Belgium, in 57 B.C. Initially this battle goes badly for the Romans, whom the Nervii have taken by surprise. Caesar says that his first task is to rally the shaken Tenth Legion, posted on the left of his battle line, after which he moves to his right wing,

> where he saw that his men were hard pressed. The soldiers were crowded too closely together to be able to fight easily, because the standards of the Twelfth Legion had been massed in one place. All the centurions of the fourth cohort had been killed, together with its standard-bearer, and its standard had been lost. In the other cohorts almost all the centurions were dead or wounded, and the chief centurion, Sextius Baculus, a very brave man, was so exhausted by the wounds, many and severe, that he had suffered that he could hardly stand up. Caesar also noticed that the rest of the soldiers in this legion were giving up the fight and that some were leaving the battle to join those in the rear ranks who were already making off. The enemy,

though advancing uphill, were maintaining the pressure on their front and at the same time pushing hard on both flanks.

The tide turns, however, when Caesar takes personal charge of this legion:

> Caesar recognised that a crisis was at hand. He had no reserves to commit, so, snatching a shield from one of the soldiers in the rear (he himself having come without one) he put himself in the front rank. Calling to the centurions by name, and shouting encouragements to the rest, he ordered them to advance the standards and deploy into extended order, so that they could use their swords more easily. His appearance brought hope to the soldiers and restored their courage. Under his eye, each man strove his utmost and the enemy's onset was checked. (Qtd. in Keegan 65)

On the surface, this account appears highly informative, paying careful attention to cause and effect: the legionaries cannot fight easily because they have crowded around their massed standards, they are demoralized because they are leaderless, they recover the will to fight when Caesar assumes their leadership, and they are able to put this will into action when Caesar spreads them out so that they can move freely. Nevertheless, as Keegan demonstrates, Caesar's account begs the same two fundamental questions about combat as Napier's description of the battle of Albuera. First, Keegan points out that Caesar depicts the combatants in oversimplified, uniform terms. The Nervii are all attacking vigorously, while all the Romans are either fighting back halfheartedly or slipping out of the battle line until Caesar—who is one of only two participants mentioned by name—arrives, at which point all the legionaries recover the will to fight. Second, Keegan notes that Caesar offers no clear explanation of precisely *how* and *why* the Romans are able to reverse their defeat, for Caesar's discussion of the battle's action is discontinuous, simply presenting three central facts—the Twelfth Legion is crumbling under the Nervii's assault, Caesar reaches the scene and spreads out the standards, the Nervii's attack loses its momentum—with no detailed account of how each action brings about the next. Exactly how, Keegan asks, does the Twelfth Legion, facing an enemy force considerably larger and already sensing victory, manage by itself to check that force's onset? Is the Romans' swordsmanship superior? Is their missile fire more accurate? Do the Nervii simply lose heart when they see the hitherto demoralized legionaries begin to recover their discipline and deploy in well-drilled fashion into open order? Caesar, Keegan emphasizes, does not say (65–66).

Despite his admiration for Caesar's work, De Forest displays neither of these battle-piece faults in his own combat writing. His explanation of the reasons for the successful charge of the Twelfth Regiment in "The First Time Under Fire" illustrates this point, but perhaps the clearest example of De Forest's attention to the very elements that Caesar fails to consider is a description in *Miss Ravenel's Conversion* of an assault by two Confederate brigades on Union Fort Winthrop, of which Colburne is second in command. De Forest presents the first part of this attack as follows:

> The [first] assailing brigade, debouching from the woods half a mile away from the Fort, had advanced in a wide front across the flat, losing scarcely any men by the fire of the [fort's] artillery, although many, shaken by the horrible screeching of the hundred-pound shells, threw themselves on the ground in the darkness or sought the frail shelter of the scattered dwellings [outside the fort's walls]. Thus diminished in numbers and broken up by night and obstacles and the differing speed of running men, the brigade reached the Fort, not an organization, but a confused swarm, flowing along the edge of the ditch to right and left in search of an entrance. There was a constant spattering of flashes as individuals returned the steady fire of the garrison; and the sharp clean whistle of round balls and buckshot mingled in the thick warm air with the hoarse whiz of Miniés. Now and then an angry shout or wailing scream indicated that some one had been hit and mangled. The exhortations and oaths of the Rebel officers could be distinctly heard as they endeavored to restore order, to drive up stragglers, and to urge the mass forward. A few jumped or fell into the ditch and floundered there, unable to climb up the smooth facings of brickwork. Two or three hundred collected around the palisade which connected the northern front with the river, some lying down and waiting, and others firing at the woodwork or the neighboring ramparts, while a few determined ones tried to burst open the gate by main strength.

. . . .

> [T]hings were going badly with the assailants. Disorganized by the night, cut up by the musketry, demoralized by the incessant screaming and bursting of the one-hundred-pound shells, unable to force the palisade or cross the ditch, they rapidly lost heart, threw themselves on the earth, took refuge behind the levees, dropped away in squads through the covering gloom, and were, in short, repulsed. In the course of thirty minutes, all that yelling swarm had disappeared except the scattered dead and wounded and a few well-covered stragglers, who continued to fire as sharpshooters. (310–12)

The differences between this description and Caesar's account of the Sambre are clear. First, De Forest does not oversimplify the attackers' behavior by presenting them as an undifferentiated charging mass. Some of the Confederates press the initial attack, but others drop out of the line to take shelter, and still others simply fall flat, paralyzed by fear. Those who continue the assault and reach the ditch act with equal individuality, some doing nothing, some returning the garrison's fire, and some trying to force the fort's gate. Second, De Forest clearly links the Confederates' individual behavior to the assault's failure, explaining that the attackers who reach the ditch cannot press onward because of their loss of numbers and organization due to fear, obstacles, different running speeds, the disorientation of darkness, and casualties.

De Forest further demonstrates superiority to Caesar in describing soldiers' behavior and outlining cause and effect in his account of the assault's next phase, the second Confederate brigade's attack. More effectively held together by its officers than the first brigade, this group reaches the ditch still a well-organized unit and begins to cross it in threatening force. Men can only remain part of a monolith for so long, however, before their unavoidable individualities of behavior reassert themselves, a fact De Forest is careful to point out and connect to the assault's failure:

> Unfortunately for the attack, the exterior slope was full of small knolls and gullies, beside being cumbered with rude shanties, of four or five feet in height made of bits of board, and shelter tents, which had served

as the quarters of the garrison. Behind these covers scores if not hundreds sought refuge and could not be induced to leave them for a second charge. They commenced with musketry, and from that moment the great peril was over. The men behind the [Union] rampart had only to lie quiet, to shoot every one who approached or rose at full length, and to wait till daylight should enable the gunboats [on the river flanking the fort] to open with grape. In vain the Rebel officers, foreseeing this danger, strove with voice and example to raise a yell and a rush. The impetuosity of the attack had died out, and could not be brought to life. (315–16)

Given this attention to individual behavior and clear explanations of its bearing on a battle's outcome, De Forest is in practice unquestionably a more realistic combat writer than Caesar. The answers to the two questions that conclude the preceding chapter are therefore more complicated than they initially seemed: De Forest used models for his military writing, but that writing is effectively realistic in spite of at least some of those models rather than because of them. Two new questions arise as a result of this insight. Why, in view of his own work's superiority, did De Forest never notice Caesar's shortcomings? And how, given his admiration for Caesar's writing, did De Forest manage to transcend its drawbacks in his own work?

The first of these questions is even more puzzling than it initially appears, for, in light of a contradiction I have not considered thus far, De Forest's blindness to Caesar's flaws seems not accidental but willful. We have seen that in *Miss Ravenel's Conversion* Dr. Ravenel praises Caesar as the best of military writers. Earlier in the novel De Forest has Colburne criticize an ancient historian's treatment of the battle of Pharsalia, fought between Caesar and Pompey in 48 B.C., as a prime example of unrevelatory battle writing. Colburne, still a civilian at this point, shortly after the war's outbreak, wonders whether he has enough of the qualities of a good soldier to rate a commission in the Union army. He makes his decision as a result of an exchange with the first professional soldier he has ever met, Lieutenant Colonel Carter, while the latter, on leave from his regiment, which is already in the field, is visiting Colburne's hometown, the New England college town of New Boston. Making conversation, Colburne notes the strength of Carter's arms and ventures that it must be the result of exercise with a sword in preparation for hand-to-hand combat. Carter replies that no modern soldier ever fights hand to hand, pointing out that "'Gunpowder has killed all that'" (29). Colburne responds by considering this information in relation to what he has learned of military matters by reading history; he concludes that the writers he has in mind have not told him everything about battle. "'Perhaps,'" he ventures to Carter, "'there never was much real hand to hand fighting. Look at the battle of Pharsalia. Two armies of Romans, the best soldiers of antiquity, meet each other, and the defeated party loses fifteen thousand men killed and wounded, while the victors lose only about two hundred. Is that fighting? Isn't it clear that Pompey's men began to run away when they got within about ten feet of Caesar's?'" (29).

This sagacity regarding historians' failure to tell the whole truth about combat prompts Carter to realize that Colburne has the makings of a capable soldier. Carter therefore persuades Colburne to enlist, promising him a commission in Carter's own regiment. That Carter, an experienced soldier, should hold a man in high esteem for suspecting most historians' treatment of battle meshes logically with the opinions De Forest himself expresses in his nonfiction about such writers. It is at the point of this connection, however, that the contradiction presents itself. In his nonfiction De Forest offers Caesar as the primary alternative to untruthful combat accounts, and in *Miss Ravenel's Conversion* he has Dr. Ravenel praising Caesar as the touchstone of effective military writing, but Caesar is the writer responsible for the unrevelatory account of Pharsalia to which Colburne refers.[2]

That Colburne and, by extension, De Forest should find this account lacking is not surprising. Leaving aside Colburne's suspicion that the account as a whole is a fiction that substitutes a battle for a massacre, it clearly partakes of the drawbacks Keegan identifies in Caesar's description of the battle of the Sambre, the same drawbacks De Forest in "Our Military Past and Future" deplores in other historians' work. Caesar's description of this battle in the *Commentaries* runs as follows:

> [O]ur men, as soon as the signal was given, charged forward with their javelins at the ready, but they noticed that the enemy were not moving forward to meet them. They then showed what they had learned

from their training and from the experience gained in previous battles. They checked their speed of their own accord and halted about halfway between the two lines, so as not to use up their energy before they reached their objective. After a short pause they went on again at the double, hurled their javelins, and then began to use their swords.

Pompey's men stood up to the attack well. They met the javelins with their shields, took the shock of the charge without breaking ranks, hurled their own javelins, and then began to use their swords. At the same moment, the cavalry on Pompey's left wing all charged together, as they had been told, and the whole mass of archers and slingers came surging around us. Our cavalry could not hold this attack and were gradually forced back and out of the way. This made Pompey's cavalry press on all the more fiercely. They now began to deploy by squadrons and to sweep around our exposed flank. Observing this, I gave the signal to the six cohorts which constituted my fourth line. They went forward immediately to the attack and fell upon Pompey's cavalry with such violence that not one of the enemy stood up to the charge; the whole lot wheeled around; it was not so much a retreat as a complete rout in which they galloped off to find safety among the highest hills in the neighborhood. Once the cavalry was out of the way, the archers and slingers, unsupported, abandoned and defenseless, were slaughtered to a man. In the main line of battle, Pompey's men were still fighting and standing firm, but my cohorts, carrying on their advance, swept around their flank and began to attack them from the rear.

It was at this moment that I ordered my third line to charge. Up to this time they had stayed in position and had not been in action. Pompey's men now found themselves attacked by an entirely fresh body of troops, who brought relief to their exhausted comrades; at the same time others were attacking them from the rear. They were unable to resist; the entire army turned and fled. (323)

Following Keegan's approach to Caesar's account of the Sambre engagement, we may legitimately subject this description to a number of observations regarding individual behavior and cause and effect. Caesar says that his troops noticed the enemy did not advance and as a result "checked their speed of their own accord." We are left to ponder the unlikelihood of *all* the soldiers' discerning this fact and acting in perfect unison, and we must similarly wonder precisely *how* this information and decision were communicated from man to man. Perhaps the officers on the scene played a role here, but Caesar does not say; his subordinates are conspicuously absent from the entire account, for reasons that will shortly become apparent. Similar objections apply to nearly all of Caesar's claims in this passage. Caesar says that when the two lines met, both sides "began to use their swords." Besides glossing over the improbability of *every* man's having done so, Caesar leaves the reader completely in the dark as to the effects of this fighting on the troops themselves, particularly on Pompey's men, who are the ones Colburne believes ran away. After this vague statement Caesar shifts immediately to another claim of uniform action, the assertion that "the cavalry on Pompey's left wing all charged together, as they had been told." Once again we must wonder if they *all* charged, and we have no idea who told them to do so. Caesar continues, "Our cavalry could not hold this attack," making no effort to explain why.

The next phase of the battle as Caesar reports it is equally mystifying. He says that his reserve infantry, acting on his orders, "went forward immediately to the attack and fell upon Pompey's cavalry with such violence that not one of the enemy stood up to the charge," but he offers not a word of explanation as to precisely how a dismounted force managed to rout a large body of more mobile horsemen who had momentum and the taste of victory in their favor. Nor does he describe how this heavily armored infantry was then able to catch up to and slaughter Pompey's more lightly clad archers and slingers, at least some of whom must have seen the battle going against them and had thoughts of escape. Finally, Caesar explains that Pompey's main line of infantrymen, still apparently "using" their swords, broke when another of Caesar's reserves fell upon them. How exactly these fresh men worked their way past their comrades, who were presumably closely engaged with Pompey's troops, is another mystery.

On the evidence of Colburne's comment on Pharsalia, De Forest seems to recognize at some level these inadequacies in Caesar's combat writing. How then can he proclaim Caesar's *Commentaries* the finest military history ever written? To begin to explain this apparent contradiction, we must go back to one of De Forest's specific reasons for praising Caesar's *Com-*

mentaries. As noted at the beginning of this chapter, in "Caesar's Art of War and of Writing" De Forest argues that Caesar is superior to Tacitus as a military historian because Caesar's accounts are free of ideology, limited to "the actual facts," whereas Tacitus' are not. What De Forest refuses to notice is that the *Commentaries* are in truth weighted with ideology from beginning to end; it is simply a different kind from that with which Tacitus concerns himself. As Keegan points out, Caesar wrote the *Commentaries* "for a carefully calculated political end": to strengthen his position in Rome by enhancing his reputation as a successful military leader (66). This self-promotion is the ideological basis of the *Commentaries*; everywhere Caesar's goal is to demonstrate that his own presence and actions are the fundamental reasons for his army's successes. This ideology is what renders the *Commentaries* unrevelatory as military history, for to make his own conduct the focus of every account of a battle Caesar has necessarily to be vague about his subordinate officers' contributions, his soldiers' individual behavior, and the ways in which these factors contribute to the legions' victories. Another look at Caesar's account of Pharsalia will illustrate this ideology and its deleterious effects on clarity.

Shortly after the battle begins, Pompey's cavalry charges and is broken, in Caesar's words, when "I gave the signal to the six cohorts which constituted my fourth line" (323). Pompey's infantry likewise gives way when "I ordered my third line to charge" (323). What stands out in these phrases is the contrast between the care Caesar takes to distinguish himself as an individual and the monolithic character he imposes on all the men under his command. Caesar speaks and his army acts. We do not see his orders relayed from his headquarters to the subordinates actually leading the units involved. We do not see, as we do in De Forest's accounts of Labadieville and the assault on Fort Winthrop, those officers struggling to maintain cohesion among their men during the advance because of individuals' various speeds. Nor do we see in Caesar's account the soldiers themselves, some running, some hesitating, some falling. The impression that Caesar gives, in fact, is that only one individual is really involved in this battle: he himself. The army becomes simply a projection of his will, an aggregate of undifferentiated automatons executing his commands and winning the victory solely as a result of their complete, unified responsiveness to those commands.

Even when Caesar ascribes some credit to the performance of his soldiers, his clear implication is that he is ultimately responsible for their actions. One reason for his troops' defeat of Pompey's, he explains, is his army's superior will to fight. He says that "there is a kind of quickening of the spirit, a sort of extra zest which is born and implanted in men by nature and which receives its great stimulus from the ardor with which they go into battle." Thus far, Caesar seems to be giving his men a share in his glory, but he returns responsibility for victory to himself with his next comment: "It is the duty of a general to encourage and not to repress this quality" (322). Since his troops won, Caesar plainly did his duty. Similarly, Caesar's report of his infantry's wisdom in slowing down and then halting of their own accord when the men realized that Pompey's men were not advancing to meet them ultimately redounds to his own credit. Caesar imputes this canny—and once again monolithic—conduct not to the insight of the officers on the scene but to the troops' training and previous experience in combat. This removal of any role for the leaders on the tactical level, coupled with the lack of any explanation of how, if the officers were not involved, every man came simultaneously to the same realization and course of action, once again makes the army simply a mass projection of Caesar's will. By referring to training and experience only in the abstract, Caesar places his emphasis not on the men directly responsible for those things but on himself as their ultimate architect.

Close study of the *Commentaries* reveals this ideology of the commander at work in every account of a battle. It explains, in particular, the lack of clarity Keegan points out in Caesar's description of the battle against the Nervii at the Sambre. For Caesar the salient point to be reported regarding this engagement is that he himself arrived on the scene and therefore all his men regained the will to fight; any explanation of how the legionaries put their new resolve into practice is unnecessary to his purpose of demonstrating his own responsibility for the victory.

This insight regarding Caesar's motives partially answers the first question I have set out to explore: we see *what* it was De Forest evidently chose to ignore in Caesar—a particular kind of ideology. However, I have not yet explained *why* he ignored it. To do so I must move ahead and consider the second question: how De Forest managed to avoid Caesar's vagueness in his own battle writing. A possible answer lies in the work of Alexander Kinglake, one of the other military writers whom De Forest mentions admiringly in "Our Military Past and Future," for this author offers a far more informative approach to combat depiction than Caesar.³ Like De Forest's work, Kinglake's *Invasion of the Crimea,* published in nine volumes between 1863 and 1887, places a primary emphasis on complex treatments of character and behavior and on coherent explanations of how these factors influence a battle's outcome. A clear example is Kinglake's narrative of the British Heavy Brigade's successful charge against a much larger force of Russian cavalry at the battle of Balaclava. Although this particular account did not appear until 1868, the year after the publication of *Miss Ravenel's Conversion,* it is characteristic of Kinglake's work as a whole, the volumes prior to 1867 as well as those after; I offer this passage despite its postdating *Miss Ravenel* because it is perhaps the most compact of many such descriptions.

First, whereas in Caesar's accounts of the Sambre and Pharsalia one man alone—Caesar—is presented as responsible for the victory and is the only figure given any individual treatment, Kinglake discusses in detail the personalities of a number of men and links their various separate actions to the Heavy Brigade's success. Before the charge began, Kinglake says, the brigade's commander, General Scarlett, had to deal with a dilemma that Caesar glosses over in his descriptions of his own behavior: whether to lead the assault in person, thus providing moral encouragement to his men but sacrificing the ability to maintain an overall grasp of the attack's conduct, or to remain behind in a supervisory role, thereby being able to respond effectively to changes in the brigade's situation as the attack developed but running the risk of damaging his troops' morale. Scarlett chose to lead the charge, Kinglake explains, but the simultaneous, independent response of Scarlett's own immediate superior, Lord Lucan, obviated any possible negative consequences of this decision. Even as Scarlett pondered his alternatives, Lucan at his headquarters learned that the Heavy Brigade was favorably positioned to make a charge and hurried to the scene to give the necessary orders, unaware that Scarlett was himself in the process of giving them. As a result of both officers' being present, Lucan was able to direct the assault from the rear while Scarlett led it from the front (136–39).

Even before his account of the charge itself begins, then, Kinglake assigns credit for its success to two officers, and he gives shares to many others for their individual bravery and leadership during the fighting, including a staff officer, Lieutenant Elliot (175–76), a squadron leader, Captain Clarke (177), and two regimental commanders, Colonels White (178) and Hodge (187). Nor are the private soldiers a mass of automatons who waver or fight only as a result of their general's absence or presence and his personal concern for their morale. Rather, Kinglake attributes the Heavy Brigade's victory largely to its inborn fighting spirit, which in his view was not simply the result of its commander's influence but derived from the brigade's consisting of two regiments that deeply respected each other, the Scots Greys and the Inniskilling Dragoons, and from both of these regiments' consisting largely of Scots and Irish, men "of the blood of those who are warriors by temperament, and not because of mere reasons" (170).

In addition to this focus on many individuals' contributions to the victory, Kinglake, unlike Caesar, takes care to explain precisely how and why a relatively small force managed to defeat a considerably greater number of opposing troops. He notes that "when a strong body of horse is hurled at full pace towards the foe, it commonly happens that either the attack or the resistance gives way before the moment of impact" (151). Such was not the case in this encounter, however, because the Russian cavalry was massed so closely together that the front ranks were physically unable to retreat before the Heavy Brigade's assault, being held in place by the ranks behind them. Kinglake then asserts that this circumstance should have led to the Heavy Brigade's defeat. Although the British troopers might logically expect to topple their opponents in the immobilized Russian front ranks, this very success would entangle them in a mass of fallen Russian horses and riders, impeding their movements, breaking them down from a unified charging line into small knots of individuals, and thus blunting their attack's initial impetus. As a result, the succeeding ranks of Russians would eventually surround and overwhelm them. That this outcome did not transpire Kinglake explains in terms of "a phenomenon so much spoken of in the days of the old war against the [Napoleonic] French Empire, that it used to be then described by a peculiar but recognised phrase" (163). This phrase is "accepting the files"; barred from retreating, the great majority of the Russians in the front ranks nevertheless chose not to meet their opponents in head-on collisions but rather yielded as much room as they could on their right or left sides and thus allowed the British to charge past them into the succeeding Russian ranks. (A direct comparison of this passage to Caesar's failure to explain how his relief troops at Pharsalia managed to work their way past their comrades to get at Pompey's men is especially illustrative of the differences between Kinglake's and Caesar's approaches to combat description.)

Even though this Russian maneuver enabled the Heavy Brigade to preserve their momentum longer than they might have initially expected, Kinglake continues, the logical outcome should nonetheless have been a British defeat, for the outnumbered brigade were only plunging farther into the enemy's mass and thus still rendering themselves liable to be slowed down and splintered into small, easily overcome groups. Kinglake is specific about why the Heavy Brigade triumphed despite this unpromising situation, offering several reasons that cover both the physical and psychological conditions of the English and Russians. Physically, he explains, the brigade's troopers were generally taller than their opponents and thus had a longer reach, a distinct advantage in hand-to-hand combat. Moreover, the Russians were unable to use their superior numbers to their benefit because for the most part they remained tightly packed together, restricting one another's movements (167–68). Psychologically, Kinglake says, the Heavy Brigade also held a considerable edge, what he calls "the unspeakable advantage of being the assailants" (171–72). The Russian cavalry was brave and well-disciplined, "but kept as they had been at a halt, and condemned (in violation of the principles which govern the use of cavalry) to be passively awaiting the attack, it was impossible for them to be comparable in ardour, self-trust, and moral ascendant [sic] to horsemen exalted and impassioned by the rapture of the charge, and now in their towering pride riding this way and that with fierce shouts through the patient long-suffering mass" (168–69).

Given its emphases on individual behavior and clarity of cause and effect and its lack of focus on the commanding general's role, this account is a model of battle writing considerably closer than Caesar's narratives to De Forest's combat descriptions. That De Forest draws on Kinglake is explicable for two reasons. First, Kinglake's attention to the contributions not just of generals but of regimental- and company-level officers as well as private soldiers accords with De Forest's personal perspective on what happens in battle, since De Forest acquired most of his firsthand experience of combat as a company commander.[4] Second, despite the somewhat patronizing tone of his ethnically based generalities about the Scots and Irish troopers, Kinglake clearly evinces a belief that every man's actions, not just the commander's, affect the outcome of a battle. Such a belief corresponds in its major points not only to De Forest's own experience but also to a larger mindset, informed by democracy, evident in much American military writing. Identifying this attitude as "a flavour . . . distinctively American," John Keegan defines it in terms of "a focus of interest upon the common soldier, rather than upon the commander, upon the acts of the majority, rather than the decisions of a few" (74). The answer to the question of how De Forest avoided Caesar's shortcomings as a combat writer in the *Commentaries* is now clear: he did so by drawing on another, more instructive source. What is still *not* clear, however, is why, given his works' closer relationship to Kinglake's than to Caesar's and his own awareness at some level of Caesar's failings, does De Forest rate Caesar the greatest military writer of all time?

The solution to this difficulty, the explanation for both De Forest's refusal truly to confront Caesar's failings as a battle writer and his own combat narratives' superiority to Caesar's, ultimately lies in the area of style. I have noted the similarity of Kinglake's content to De Forest's; what I have not noted is the considerable difference in their styles. A glance at the last few lines of Kinglake's account of the Heavy Brigade's charge, as quoted above, will prove instructive. Here, in Kinglake's description of the "ardour, self-trust, and moral ascendant" of the Scots and Irish troopers, "exalted and impassioned by the rapture of the charge, and now in their towering pride riding this way and that with fierce shouts through the patient long-suffering mass" (168–69), is a dramatic floridity that stands in marked contrast to De Forest's straightforward, unadorned approach, as in his description of his men at the moment of their victory at Labadieville. At the sight of the Confederates' retreat, De Forest says, the Union troops "trampled . . . smack up to the cypress fence [behind which the Confederates had been entrenched], yelling with delight and blazing away at the woods, although the enemy had vanished like a dream. It was all that the officers could do to halt the excited men and put an end to their riotous shouting" (*Volunteer's Adventures* 67).

Where Kinglake's high-flown diction and elaborate building up of modifying phrases create a heroic image for his subjects that is much like Tennyson's depiction of the Light Brigade in the same battle as "victors and lords," De Forest's diction, to the extent that it creates any mediating image at all, characterizes his men as more like rowdy children, in simpler sentences that accord with this antiromantic sense, with both of these features correlating with his assertion that "Caesar never 'bears on' and never struts, not even when he is relating sublime deeds of heroism" ("Caesar's Art" 288).

Kinglake's grandiosity of style, like Caesar's simplicity, from which De Forest's derives, can be explained in terms of ideology. Like Caesar, Kinglake writes from a specific ideological standpoint; the difference is that Kinglake's ideology is largely the opposite of Caesar's. Because Caesar seeks only to emphasize his own role in his battles, he is wary of large-scale imagery and metaphors that might call attention to his troops. Kinglake's goal, on the other hand, is to glorify the troops along with the commanders, and the most direct way of doing so, especially for a mid-nineteenth-century audience familiar with romantic prose, is to encode their actions in hyperbolic language. Indeed, if Caesar may be said to have imposed the "cult of the commander" on much military literature, Kinglake may equally be said to be in thrall to another literary-historical cult, that of the unconquerable British soldier, of the gallant "thin red line," to use an image that encapsulates this ideology's devotion to figures of speech.

With these facts in mind, it is useful to consider Napier's work and De Forest's opinion of it. Napier's description of the climax of the battle of Albuera, which appeared in full in the opening section of this study, although far less specific about individual behavior and cause and effect than Kinglake's work (the reasons Keegan finds Napier's account typical of the battle-piece at its worst), is in style strikingly like the passage from Kinglake quoted above. A consideration of content in connection with style in part of this description will demonstrate that this similarity is a result of Napier's likewise writing out of the ideology of the invincible British soldier. Napier reports that at the beginning of the Fusilier Brigade's advance,

> Myers [the brigade commander] was killed, Cole, the three colonels, Ellis, Blakeney, and Hawkshawe [the four officers directly below Myers in the chain of command], fell wounded, and the fusilier battalions,

struck by the iron tempest, reeled and staggered like sinking ships. But suddenly and sternly recovering, they closed on their terrible enemies, and then was seen with what strength and majesty the British soldier fights.... Nothing could stop that astonishing infantry. No sudden burst of undisciplined valour, no nervous enthusiasm weakened the stability of their order, their flashing eyes were bent on the dark columns in their front, their measured tread shook the ground, their dreadful volleys swept away the head of every formation, their deafening shouts overpowered the dissonant cries that broke from all parts of the tumultuous crowd, as slowly and with a horrid carnage it was pushed by the incessant vigour of the attack to the farthest edge of the height. There the French reserve, mixing with the struggling multitude, endeavoured to restore the fight but only augmented the irremediable disorder, and the mighty mass giving way like a loosened cliff, went headlong down the steep: the rain flowed after in streams discoloured with blood, and eighteen hundred unwounded men, the remnant of six thousand unconquerable British soldiers, stood triumphant on the fatal hill. (Qtd. in Keegan 37–38)

The connection of a hyperbolic style to the achievements of the British soldier in this passage is obvious; what we might observe in addition is that Napier goes even further than Kinglake in sharing the credit for the attack's success between the commanders and the troops. In fact, in noting that virtually the entire chain of command was incapacitated at the attack's outset, Napier seems to eschew any notion of leaders' roles as important; the victory appears to depend entirely on the British private soldier's discipline and natural will to fight.

Once we understand Napier's devotion to the contributions of the common soldier, De Forest's admiration for his work despite its overgenerality and lack of clarity regarding cause and effect makes sense. But however closely related De Forest's content may be to Kinglake's and Napier's, his style is far closer to Caesar's straightforward approach than to the Englishmen's romantic extravagance, as Edmund Wilson suggests in his reference to De Forest's "Roman impassivity" (650). De Forest's descriptions are explicit in the manner of Kinglake, yet, as we have seen in "The First Time Under Fire" and the assault on the fort from *Miss Ravenel's*

Conversion, they are also, in the manner of Caesar, far more restrained in terms of mediating imagery. As Albert E. Stone points out, De Forest, almost alone among authors writing about the Civil War shortly after its end, "allow[s] his mighty subject to provide the emotion for the events; he has dispensed with the language of metaphor" (87).⁵ What De Forest's combat writing does, then, is combine Kinglake's and Napier's devotion to the average soldier and Kinglake's emphasis on the details of combat with Caesar's style; what this combination suggests is that in Kinglake's work De Forest found ideas about what happened to soldiers in battle that corresponded to his own experience, but in these writings by a civilian he did not find those facts presented in a soldier's manner.

Let us recall De Forest's reasons for praising Caesar's *Commentaries*. In *Miss Ravenel's Conversion* De Forest has Dr. Ravenel laud the *Commentaries* for "'precision, brevity, elegance, and every other classical quality of style'" (207), and in "Caesar's Art of War and of Writing" De Forest speaks admiringly of Caesar's style for its "[e]xtreme simplicity and naturalness" (287) and lack of "points and artifices of rhetoric" (288). The crucial fact for understanding De Forest's motives for combining Kinglake and Caesar is his explanation of the source of this style: "the great soldier is by birthright a clear and quick thinker, and his literary utterance is naturally a reflex of his mental operations" (288). What De Forest does in this passage, in effect, is to establish one criterion for the writings of a good soldier; and by this criterion a straightforward style in turn becomes a validation of the author's military skill. Caesar, however, violates De Forest's other major tenet of good battle writing, the necessity of focusing specifically on what really happens to men engaged in combat. De Forest himself wishes to tell more of the facts than Caesar does, but he wishes to do so in a voice that says that he, like Caesar, is a capable soldier. And so, having established the style in which a such a soldier writes, De Forest adopts this manner for himself, despite the shortcomings of the content beneath this manner in its original source.

The two questions this chapter set out to explore have been answered, then: De Forest avoided Caesar's shortcomings in his own writing because he leavened his personal experience of combat with literary models more revelatory than Caesar's, but he maintains Caesar's superiority because of his commitment to the idea of the great soldier as a classically simple writer.

Perhaps one more question merits exploration at this point, the sources of this commitment. The answer seems to reside in the ultimate disappointment that De Forest encountered in his military career. Commissioned a captain of volunteers at the beginning of this career, on 1 January 1862, De Forest intended to rise in the ranks and attain a place for himself in the postwar regular army. However, he found himself well down on the seniority list and lacking in political connections, the two most direct routes to promotion and regular status. Therefore, despite being frequently mentioned in dispatches for gallantry, he was mustered out of the service exactly six years later at only one rank higher, as "a disappointed brevet major," in Thomas F. O'Donnell's words (580).[6] That this lack of acknowledgment rankled De Forest is clear, for a note of bitterness is still unmistakable in his attitude more than thirty years later. Edwin Oviatt notes in his 1898 interview with the writer that he began by addressing De Forest as "Colonel," to which De Forest tartly responded, "'I am not a Colonel. I know that I am known as 'Colonel,' but I never received such a high rank. I suppose that they call me that because I have lived a great deal in the South, where everybody is a 'Colonel'" (40).

De Forest's writing can be seen as an implicit rejoinder to this frustration. Asserting a link between straightforward prose and military achievement in "Caesar's Art of War and of Writing," De Forest tacitly invites the reader to judge the rest of his writing by this standard; through his own straightforward prose, he demonstrates that he was a good soldier, despite the army's failure fully to acknowledge that fact. To write well about war is to prove that he served well in war, his lack of a genuine colonelcy notwithstanding.[7]

Given Caesar's shortcomings and De Forest's devotion to Caesar, it would seem that De Forest should have fallen headlong into Harold Frederic's trap. Instead, he avoids it by not copying his source but rather by adhering to the idea he believes underlies that source, a soldierly devotion to directness and clarity. Through his own experiences he learned much about what war was, and in his blending of Kinglake with Caesar he developed a form for conveying those experiences in a way that transcended the separate failings of those influences.

Part III

Ambrose Bierce

CHAPTER 6

The Failures of History

Determining whether Ambrose Bierce avoided Harold Frederic's trap of writing in accordance with other authors' depictions of war rather than out of his own experience is more difficult than in De Forest's case, for Bierce offers few clues about his influences. In his long postwar writing career he made very few statements concerning the military writers he admired, nothing so comprehensive as De Forest's listings in "Our Military Past and Future" and "Caesar's Art of War and of Writing." As Napier Wilt points out, in all his Civil War pieces Bierce mentions only three works by other authors—the memoirs of Generals William T. Sherman and William B. Hazen and an article by General O. O. Howard about Sherman's Atlanta campaign (270)—and he has little to say about combat literature, at least in the way of positive comments about specific authors, anywhere else.[1] At least two critics, Eric Solomon ("Bitterness" 193–94) and Larzer Ziff (168), after unfruitful attempts at identifying sources, have gone so far as to conclude that Bierce had no influences on his war writing, that he completely invented his own form.

Such extreme statements are arguable, given that Bierce, although he was only eighteen when he enlisted in the Ninth Indiana Infantry in 1861, was already familiar, as Hartley Grattan has shown, with a number of books in his father's library that contained descriptions of battles, including the *Iliad, Vanity Fair, Les Misérables,* and several of Walter Scott's novels (126); that he had had at least a smattering of military education in 1859 at the Kentucky Military Institute; and that Lars Ahnebrink has identified in several stories a debt to Tolstoy's *Sebastopol.*[2] Nevertheless, combing Bierce's combat literature for evidence of particular authors' influence and transcendence of that influence is less illuminating than performing the same process with the more forthcoming De Forest. A strategy of greater promise with Bierce is to look not for assessments of what good combat writing is but rather for opinions on what it is not, since he is comparatively expansive in this area, indulging fairly frequently in sneering dismissals of authors who write about "forts, guns and warships without having observed them, and battles without having seen one" (qtd. in *Skepticism* 35). Such a remark inevitably recalls De Forest's condemnation of battle accounts by men who "'did not know a manoeuvre from a hole in the ground'" ("Recent Literature" 406), and indeed the most profitable way to approach Bierce's criticisms is to return momentarily to De Forest, since an examination of certain connections between these two writers sharply illuminates Bierce's attitude toward influences and, ultimately, his vision of war.

The discussion in the preceding chapter of De Forest's transcendence of the ideologies inherent in his influences, coupled with the critics' general praise for his realism as quoted extensively in chapter 4, might be taken to imply that De Forest's own work attains its high degree of accuracy because, unlike its models, it is free of all ideology. To make such a claim, however, would be to commit the same error De Forest himself makes in his judgment that Caesar's *Commentaries* attains realism through a refusal of ideological considerations. As recent literary theoreticians have profitably reminded us (although the essential idea of course goes back at least as far as Aristotle), all writing, whether history, criticism, fiction, or any other form, as the product of a limited, selecting human intelligence, necessarily proceeds from some kind of ideological framework. Early on in his introductory volume on literary theory, for instance, Terry Eagleton notes that "[t]o speak of 'literature and ideology' as two separate phenomena which can be interrelated is . . . in one sense quite unnecessary. Literature, in the meaning of the word we have inherited, *is* ideology" (22). We can be relatively certain that at some level De Forest himself understood this point, understood the inevitably subjective quality of his own vision of combat, despite his ignoring of Caesar's ideology of the commander manifested in his assertion that Caesar presented only the objective facts, if we recall from this study's third chapter his remarks to William Dean Howells regarding all literature's being a "selection" from life rather than the entirety of it. "[W]e cannot tell the whole [of] life," De Forest says. "Let each one select what he can best paint" (qtd. in Light 167). In my third chapter, following Jackson K. Putnam's lead, I drew a distinction between a literary work's "facts" and its "truth"—facts being the objectively verifiable actions, thoughts, and feelings contained in a text and truth being the higher meaning, the "moral and emotional significance," in Putnam's words (17), that the author subjectively derives from those facts. If De Forest knows he cannot include all the facts about battle, then what version of the "truth," in Putnam's sense of the word, does he tell? Putting the question another way, by what principles does De Forest "select," to use his own term, the facts he does include, and what moral and emotional significance does he attach to those facts? To answer these questions, let us determine what De Forest's ideology is and look at the ways in which that ideology informs what De Forest reports and how he reports it.

 The ground point of De Forest's ideology is his belief, as illustrated in the previous chapter, that the successful soldier is also a lucid writer; as De Forest says in "Our Military Past and Future," this soldier is able to convey the objectively verifiable facts about what goes on in battle in a way that enables the reader to grasp "just what war is" and to see cause and effect in the outcomes of specific battles. The primary value of such military men's writings, in De Forest's opinion, is that they prepare the neophyte soldier for what he will encounter in combat. De Forest emphasizes that the nature of battle is such that the man under fire has very little comprehension of his circumstances and, lacking some accurate preconceptions about what to do in such a situation, he is liable to break down into disorientation and panic. Honestly and clearly written battle accounts, De Forest concludes, give him those saving preconceptions (567–71).

De Forest does not merely state this formula as a theory in this prescriptive article; he also demonstrates it in action in both his fiction and his memoirs. In the section of *Miss Ravenel's Conversion* devoted to the Union's siege of the Confederate stronghold at Port Hudson, in an episode very similar to one of De Forest's own experiences during the siege, as recounted in *A Volunteer's Adventures,* Captain Colburne is awakened at five o'clock one morning and ordered to prepare his company for action. No one informs him whether he will take part in an assault on the fortress or a defense against a Confederate sally, nor is he told whether his regiment, which is all he can see in the dense forest around the fort, will have the support of other Union troops. As for the enemy's location, Colburne only gets an idea when artillery shells and musket balls start to tear through the trees above and around him and the leading figures of what becomes a steady stream of wounded straggle toward him. Rather than helping Colburne orient himself, this discovery of the enemy's position only heightens the stresses he feels, for a moment later several of his own men fall wounded and his company begins to dissolve into the disorder preceding rout as the unwounded drop out of their places in the line of battle to help the stricken. At this critical juncture, the understanding of military history and principles that led Colonel Carter to offer Colburne a commission to begin with enables him to recover the situation. He calls to mind the fundamental military principle, as stated in the Army Regulations, that "'[s]oldiers must not be permitted to leave the ranks . . . to assist the wounded unless by express permission, which is only to be given after the action is decided. The highest interest and most pressing duty is to win the victory, by which only can a proper care of the wounded be ensured'" (263). Armed with this precept, Colburne commands that the wounded be made comfortable in the shade and that all the unwounded remain on the battle line, and he thereby restores order. Colburne's sense of an officer's responsibilities, implanted by his understanding of military history and the tactical principles derived from it, thus enables him to remain rational and effective in a most irrational situation.

In De Forest's nonfiction we might recall a similar incident in "The

First Time Under Fire," one I briefly discussed in my fourth chapter. Here De Forest depicts himself, like Colburne, concentrating in a moment of stress on his obligation as an officer to keep himself from breaking down into alienation and isolation, his obligation to remain rational and in touch with other men and thus effective on the battlefield. As De Forest leads his company toward the enemy's position at Labadieville, he sees his first wounded man. His description of this figure evokes horror—the man is "a ghastly sufferer, his knee crushed by a shot, his torn trowsers soaked with a dirty crimson, his eyes looking the agony of death" (477)—but simultaneously De Forest feels an immediate sense of his responsibility to keep up his troops' morale, a sense that keeps him from becoming preoccupied with his own revulsion at the sight. "I did not want my men to see this dismaying spectacle," he explains, "and called their attention to something, I have forgotten what, which was passing on the other side of the bayou" (477).

Considering these incidents in light of De Forest's conception of the good soldier as good writer evinces the central "truth" of De Forest's Civil War work: despite its undeniable horrors—a terrifying lack of understanding of one's circumstances and the imminent prospect of ghastly wounds and sudden death—battle is rationally assimilable and intellectually manageable for the individual combatant through a recourse to history, whether that history is presented on its own or embedded in a work of fiction. This is of course not to suggest that De Forest regards all history as reliable and useful, for his lambasting of "ignorant romancers calling themselves historians" in "Our Military Past and Future" attests otherwise. Rather, the history he has in mind is that written by knowledgeable military men, because such works enable the soldier to put his experiences into a historical context, to see his feelings in a larger perspective, and thus to avoid isolating himself in immediate subjective responses. Through this constant awareness that his experience in war is not unique but rather part of a long tradition that offers an intellectual framework and lessons on what to do, the soldier wards off the feelings of alienation and aloneness that are natural to his circumstances.[3] Like Colburne and De Forest himself, the good soldier prepares for the experience of battle by reading combat literature; the understanding of the history of warfare he gains thereby enables him to function effectively in battle; and, because of his rationality under fire, he is subsequently able to recall enough of his experience to write his own accurate account that contributes to the body of knowledge future soldiers will draw on—a cycle De Forest sees himself completing in his own memoirs and fiction.

That this view of history as a means for understanding and coping with one's present experiences under fire is De Forest's central truth is borne out by the fact that through frequent historical allusions—usually to the classical period, which is not surprising, given his admiration for Caesar—the action of both *Miss Ravenel's Conversion* and *A Volunteer's Adventures* unfolds in the perspective of and as part of the continuum of military history. De Forest has Dr. Ravenel, in addition to comparing Colburne's accounts of battles to Caesar's work, liken the Union's war effort to a Roman endeavor. Watching Federal troops arrive in New Orleans, Ravenel thinks of the Union's Armies of the Potomac and the Cumberland simultaneously operating on two other fronts and is moved to exclaim, "'It is a most glorious spectacle, this exhibition of the power of the Republic. One is absolutely reminded of consular Rome, carrying on the war with Hannibal in Italy, and at the same time sending one great army to Spain and another to North Africa'" (214). This historical consciousness underlies even small moments; De Forest says in the ninth chapter of *A Volunteer's Adventures,* "After Port Hudson," that his men have erected a board shanty for him and jokes that "I am afraid I shall get demoralized by so much luxury, like Hannibal's army at Capua" (152).

Two other such allusions are particularly striking for passing through the classical realm and into the mythological. Recalling at one point in the version of "The First Time Under Fire" included in *A Volunteer's Adventures* his entire regiment's prompt obedience to a command to lie down, De Forest says that after the battle no one can discover who gave this order. "It certainly was not given by our commander," he notes, "for we presently heard him yelling, 'Forward, Twelfth!'" Upon reflection, De Forest decides that as much explanation as is possible is that the event puts him in mind of "those godlike voices which resounded in ancient battles, giving encouragement or spreading panic" (65). Similarly, in his account in *A Volunteer's Adventures* of the opening stages of the battle of Cedar Creek, in which the Union army of General Philip Sheridan was demoralized and forced to retreat from its lines by a surprise attack by Confederate forces under General Jubal Early, De Forest says that "[t]here was panic in the air; I was conscious of that strange, depressing epidemic which the ancients attributed to a god; it seemed to me that the whole army was scared" (216). In these allusions, De Forest seems to aim, whether consciously or not, at the largest and strongest possible historical context for his experience and, by extension, for that of the future soldiers who will read his work as preparation for combat. As Roland Barthes defines the term, a myth "purifies [historical conditions], it makes them innocent, it gives them a natural and eternal justification, it gives them a clarity which is not that of an explanation but that of a statement of fact" (143). Thus, however bizarre or unsettling those future soldiers may initially find similar experiences of their own, they will be saved from terror and isolation, and ultimately enabled to continue functioning, by the realization that those experiences are part of natural and eternal phenomena.

This treatment of history and myth as stabilizing influences for men in battle also explains De Forest's failure to select one particular set of "facts" as part of his "truth" in *Miss Ravenel's Conversion,* a failure that Solomon identifies in his criticism that, where the fears of soldiers are concerned, De Forest provides only "the frightened reactions of a few hastily sketched figures" (*Banners* 192). De Forest himself notes this defect in an 1887 letter to Howells detailing his reactions to his first reading of *War and Peace.* In a passage Howells quoted in the May 1887 issue of *Harper's,* De Forest admits that Tolstoy gives a fuller picture of combat than he himself did in *Miss Ravenel's Conversion:* "Let me tell you that nobody but [Tolstoy] has written the whole truth about war and battle. *I* tried and told all that I dared, and perhaps all I could, but there was one thing I did not dare tell, lest the world should infer that I was naturally a coward, and so could not know the feelings of a brave man. I actually did not dare state the extreme horror of battle and the anguish with which the bravest soldiers struggle through it" (987).

De Forest's putative fears of being thought a coward obviously tally on the surface with what I have said about his conception of his writing as proof of his having been a good soldier, but it should be carefully noted that he says he is not merely afraid of being thought a coward but, by extension, of being regarded as one who cannot know—and thus cannot provide information about—how a brave man feels under fire. This assertion suggests that his omission ties in more deeply with his sense of himself as a soldier-writer within the historical cycle, as a conveyor of accurate but also useful examples—as a conveyor, in other words, of not only facts but also truth. For De Forest, the truth beneath the facts of combat, as contained in two thousand years of military history and confirmed by his own experience, is that the brave man does quail before the horror of the battlefield, but this feeling is in itself less important than his constructive response to it, and so it is the latter rather than the former that he should focus on, not only when he is on the battlefield but also when he is writing about that horror and response after the fact with the intent of imparting to others useful principles about what to do in the midst of battle. It is noteworthy in this regard that none of the authors De Forest praises in "Our Military Past and Future" for producing "practical and instructive" (573) books on combat dwells on battle's horror and anguish any more extensively than does De Forest. It is even more significant that, his self-accusatory tone to Howells concerning *Miss Ravenel's Conversion* notwithstanding, in *A Volunteer's Adventures* De Forest does not gloss over the fact that brave men feel fear under fire but confirms it and seeks to explain why most do not give way to it. Meditating on the sort of behavior he exhibited when he encountered the wounded man at Labadieville, and when he led the charge later in the same battle, he explains that "officers are in general braver than soldiers" because the private soldier "is responsible for himself alone, and so is apt to think of himself alone. The officer is responsible for his company, and so partially forgets his own peril. His whole soul is occupied with the task of keeping his ranks in order, and it is only now and then that he takes serious note of the bullets and shells. It would demand a good deal of courage, I think to be a mere looker-on in battle" (75).

Similarly, De Forest recalls that at one point during the siege of Port Hudson the Union commander, General Nathaniel Banks, ordered his already battle-weary troops to conduct a "nocturnal reconnaissance on a grand scale" (124). Knowing that the Confederate positions were strongly fortified and that their own ranks had been severely thinned by two weeks of fighting, De Forest says, he and his fellow-officers regarded Banks's orders as "simple madness," but, recollecting their responsibilities as officers, they "[o]f course . . . prepared to obey them," in their turn giving their men orders that "the cartridge boxes . . . be replenished, the canteens and haversacks filled, and the blankets slung. That is to say, we got ready to occupy the enemy's position precisely as if we expected to carry it" (125).

It is experiences such as these that illustrate and support De Forest's contention that "[t]he man who does not dread to die or to be mutilated is a lunatic. The man who, dreading these things, still faces them for the sake of duty and honor is a hero" (124). In light of these comments, perhaps a more specific phrasing of the central "truth" of De Forest's war writing offered earlier—that through a recourse to history the individual combatant can rationally assimilate and intellectually manage the horrors of battle—is in order: one can only survive battle's horror, De Forest ultimately says, by doing as he did when he saw the wounded man at Labadieville, as he depicts both Colburne and himself doing during the attacks on Port Hudson, and as he does in recounting those events in his texts: thinking of something else—namely, his historically defined duty as an officer.

The issue of horror unconfronted or marginalized brings us to Bierce, since, even if a reader knows only very little about Bierce's Civil War memoirs and stories, he or she is likely to be aware that these pieces never fail to confront horror but, rather, fairly bristle with it; they are "replete with disgusting ugliness," in Eric Solomon's phrase ("Bitterness" 182). Perhaps the best way to begin with Bierce, however, is with the similarities between his writings and De Forest's rather than with their differences, since the similarities lie on the surface level of objectively observable facts (which means that Bierce's observations as treated over the next several pages also correspond to the findings of the combat historians discussed in the first chapter two chapters of this study), while the differences reside at a deeper level, that regarding the "truth" or "moral significance" each writer derives from his facts. If we recall De Forest's insistence that the soldier knows almost nothing about the relationship of his position on the battlefield to the larger strategic picture, then we will find something familiar in Bierce's caveat in one of his memoirs, "The Crime at Pickett's Mill," that follows an explanation of the opposing armies' positions:

> The civilian reader must not suppose when he reads accounts of military operations in which relative position[s] of the forces are defined, as in the foregoing passages, that these were matters of general knowl-

> edge to those engaged. Such statements are commonly made, even by those high in command, in the light of later disclosures, such as the enemy's official reports. It is seldom, indeed, that a subordinate officer knows anything about the disposition of the enemy's forces—except that it is unamiable—or precisely whom he is fighting. As to the rank and file, they can know nothing more of the matter than the arms they carry. They hardly know what troops are upon their own right or left the length of a regiment away. If it is a cloudy day they are ignorant even of the points of the compass. It may be said, generally, that a soldier's knowledge of what is going on around him is coterminous with his official relation to it and his personal connection with it; what is going on in front of him he does not know at all until he learns it afterward. (39)

Bierce's account in the same memoir of his brigade's assault on the Confederate right in the engagement at Pickett's Mill also inevitably recalls De Forest's work, specifically, his descriptions of the demeanor of infantry in combat, since, like De Forest, Bierce dwells on the discontinuities created by natural obstacles and physical and mental inequalities among the attackers. Troops in an attack, De Forest says, advance "not in solid masses, but in fragile groups or slender lines, swaying backwards and forwards unexpectedly, gaping open here and there with slaughter or sudden quailing" ("Military Past" 572). Bierce reports that when his brigade moved forward on the attack,

> In less than one minute the trim battalions had become simply a swarm of men struggling through the undergrowth of the forest, pushing and crowding. The front was irregularly serrated, the strongest and bravest in advance, the others following in fan-like formations, variable and inconstant, ever defining themselves anew. For the first two hundred yards our course lay along the left bank of a small creek in a deep ravine, our left battalions sweeping along its steep slope. Then we came to the fork of the ravine. A part of us crossed below, the rest above, passing over both branches, the regiments inextricably intermingled, rendering all military formation impossible. (43)

A third point of similarity between Bierce's work and De Forest's is Bierce's determination to provide detailed explanations for battles' outcomes, explanations of the sort De Forest insists on in "Our Military Past and Future" and which, as we have seen in "The First Time Under Fire" and *Miss Ravenel's Conversion,* he consistently provides. The fundamental reason for the failure of his brigade's assault, Bierce says, is that this force numbered fewer than fifteen hundred men and yet its corps commander, General O. O. Howard, ordered it to attack a position defended by nearly six thousand Confederates. (Howard's order is the "crime" of the piece's title.) But Bierce, like De Forest in "The First Time Under Fire," is not content simply with this sort of large-scale answer. Just as De Forest explains that at Labadieville his regiment kept up a steady file-fire while it advanced and thus prevented the Confederates from firing effectively in response, Bierce offers a highly detailed account of what happened during the assault that caused his brigade to falter. "Early in my military experience," he says,

> I used to ask myself how it was that brave troops could retreat while still their courage was high. As long as a man is not disabled he can go forward; can it be anything but fear that makes him stop and finally retire? Are there signs by which he can infallibly know the struggle to be hopeless? In this engagement, as in others, my doubts were answered as to the fact; the explanation is still obscure. In many instances which have come under my observation, when hostile lines of infantry engage at close range and the assailants afterward retire, there was a "dead-line" beyond which no man advanced but to fall. Not a soul of them ever reached the enemy's front to be bayoneted or captured. It was a matter of the difference of three or four paces—too small a distance to affect the accuracy of aim. In these affairs no aim is taken at individual antagonists; the soldier delivers his fire at the thickest mass in his front. The fire is, of course, as deadly at twenty paces as at fifteen; at fifteen as at ten. Nevertheless, there is the "dead-line," with its well-defined edge of corpses—those of the bravest. Where both lines are fighting without cover—as in a charge met by a counter-charge—each has its "dead-line," and between the two is a clear space—neutral ground, devoid of dead, for the living cannot reach it to fall there.

> I observed this phenomenon at Pickett's Mill. Standing at the right of the line I had an unobstructed view of the narrow, open space across which the two lines fought.... Of the "hundreds of corpses within twenty paces of the Confederate line" [Bierce quotes from another report of the battle], I venture to say that a third were within fifteen paces, and not one within ten.
>
> It is the perception—perhaps unconscious—of this inexplicable phenomenon that causes the still unharmed, still vigorous and still courageous soldier to retire without having come into actual contact with his foe. He sees, or feels, that he cannot. His bayonet is a useless weapon for slaughter; its purpose is a moral one. Its mandate exhausted, he sheathes it and trusts to the bullet.[4] That failing, he retreats. He has done all that he could do with such appliances as he has.
>
> No command to fall back was given, none could have been heard. Man by man, the survivors withdrew at will, sifting through the trees into the cover of the ravines, among the wounded who could draw themselves back; among the skulkers whom nothing could have dragged forward. (45–47)

Clearly, regarding the kinds of facts that should be reported about what happens in battle, Bierce is in close agreement with De Forest. It is not surprising, therefore, that numerous critics praise Bierce's Civil War writings for realism of detail just as they do De Forest's, noting in Richard O'Connor's words, that Bierce's work contains "no gallant charges, no guidons flying or trumpets blowing, none of the usual muralistic trappings of war literature" (164).[5] Once these resemblances on the level of objective observation have been enumerated, however, the differences between De Forest's work and Bierce's become more apparent than the similarities, since what is then immediately discernible is a divergence in the attitudes De Forest and Bierce take toward their facts. And here is where the issue of horror attains significance, for the salient point of difference between these attitudes is that while De Forest refuses to dwell extensively on battle's ghastliness, Bierce often seems to focus on nothing else. Consider once more, for instance, De Forest's description in "The First Time Under Fire" of his first sight of a wounded man: "his knee crushed by a shot, his torn trowsers soaked with a dirty crimson, his face a ghastly yellow, his eyes looking the agony of death." As I have noted, this account is direct and unflinching, but it is not elaborately vivid. Compare it to Bierce's account of his confrontation with a wounded man in the memoir "What I Saw of Shiloh." Working his way toward the battle line, Bierce says, he encountered "a Federal sergeant, variously hurt, who had been a fine giant in his time. He lay face upward, taking in his breath in convulsive, rattling snorts, and blowing it out in sputters of froth which crawled creamily down his cheeks, piling itself alongside his neck and ears. A bullet had clipped a groove in his skull, above the temple; from this the brain protruded in bosses, dropping off in flakes and strings" (22–23).

De Forest and Bierce obviously saw much the same sight, aside from the wound's location, but they report it in an entirely different manner. De Forest is brisk and matter-of-fact. The awfulness of the sight registers with him, but he refuses to dwell on it, having other issues—particularly his men's morale—to consider. Bierce, on the other hand, allows this sight to override all other concerns; the wealth of detail, arresting the reader with its ghastliness, likewise stops Bierce the observer in his physical and mental tracks. Neither De Forest nor Bierce evinces any compassion for the wounded man, but where De Forest represents himself as remaining in touch with his own men and his responsibilities to them, Bierce depicts his response to this sight as an impulse to isolate himself from both the casualty and the men in his charge by indulging in brutal jokes at the expense of the injured man and one of his own shaken soldiers. Having described the stricken sergeant's lobes dropping from his skull, Bierce refuses any sympathy with the sarcastic comment that "I had not previously known one could get on, even in this unsatisfactory fashion, with so little brain" (23).[6] Regarding his relationship to his own men, the sight impels Bierce not to consider its effects on their morale or to think about what regulations prescribe in the way of conduct toward the wounded, but to make harsh sport of their unsteady responses. "One of my men whom I knew for a womanish fellow," Bierce explains, "asked if he should put his bayonet through [the dying sergeant]. Inexpressibly shocked by his cold-blooded proposal, I told him I thought not; it was unusual, and too many were looking" (23).

Both of these reactions accord with Elaine Scarry's research on battle. She asserts that when a soldier encounters a wounded man, when he is "confronted by the open body itself," he "does not have the option of failing to perceive its reality that rushes unstoppably across his eyes and into his mind, yet the mind so flees from what it sees that it will with almost equal speed perform the countermovement of assigning that attribute to something else, especially if there is something else at hand made ready to receive the rejected attribute, ready to act as its referent" (126). This countermovement, Scarry explains elsewhere, normally proceeds in one of six possible directions: the "centrality of the act of injuring" in war can simply be omitted; it can be "held in a visible but marginal position" by any of four metaphorical routes that subordinate it to the larger goal of winning; or through imagery it can be "redescribed" in such a way as to render the wounded man or men less than human (80). Plainly, De Forest chooses one of the metaphorical routes, displacing his attention from the physical wound to the psychical wound it poses to the morale of his men, while Bierce takes the path of redescription. And this divergence is paradigmatic of the difference between De Forest's and Bierce's visions of war: it reveals in essence the different "truth" that each writer derives from what is basically the same set of facts.

For De Forest the truth is that history makes the individual's experience of battle intellectually manageable, and his response to wounding falls within this framework. Bierce's view of history, on the other hand, is pithily expressed in his definition of this word in his *Devil's Dictionary:* "An account mostly false, of events mostly unimportant, which are brought about by rulers mostly knaves, and soldiers mostly fools" (51). The truth of his combat writing is likewise that history is nearly always false and that, because it therefore provides no usable perspective or context for the neophyte in combat, a soldier cannot rationally assimilate his experience. Thus, the essence of the individual's experience is always what Bierce depicts himself undergoing at Shiloh: a nightmare of ignorance, irrationality, and horror to which the only possible response is subjective, leading inevitably to the alienation and isolation he evinces in his response to wounding. The best a "truthful" combat writer can do is document this process, not mitigate it; such mitigation, the presentation of combat as intellectually manageable, as less than overwhelmingly horrifying, is the mark of a writer who falsifies the experience—is the mark of history as it is usually written. Thus, Bierce discerns a cycle of military-historical writing almost precisely the opposite of the one De Forest envisions. De Forest sees novice soldiers reading works by earlier soldiers that acknowledge but minimize the fog and terror of battle; these soldiers are thus able to withstand the stresses of combat, and then they in their turn document this process for ensuing generations. Bierce sees the minimizing in combat accounts not as practical but as pernicious, proceeding negatively, egotistically, from the writers' desire, as expressed by De Forest in his letter to Howells, not to be regarded as cowards and, as in Bierce's definition, as the fools that they in fact are; this minimizing results first in the readers' breaking down in combat themselves due to their lack of preparedness for the full extent of battle's fog and terror, and then, if they happen to survive, in their falsifying this experience in their own turn to avoid being adjudged cowards, thereby setting the next generation up for the same failure. To demonstrate Bierce's formulation and development of this truth, I will devote the rest of this chapter and much of the next to examining the opinions on military history Bierce expresses in some of his criticism, memoirs, and short stories, and to tracing the way these opinions shape the meanings of a number of other short stories and memoirs. I will look first at his view of how and why history is false, and then I will take up his depictions of the effects of its falsity on its readers.

Bierce made most of his judgments regarding the defects of military history in his weekly column in the *San Francisco Examiner,* particularly from 1898 to 1899, the period of the Spanish-American War. Because of his well-known distinguished service in the Civil War, including citations and promotions from private to first lieutenant for valor at the battles of Missionary Ridge and Kennesaw Mountain, his editors and publisher, William Randolph Hearst, considered him their most qualified writer on military subjects, and so during the Spanish-American conflict they encouraged him to devote at least part of each column to the current battles in Cuba and the Philippines. Bierce responded with acerbic skepticism about every aspect of the war, from its motivations to its conduct to its consequences, but he was especially biting about the reports war correspondents and artists sent back from the front lines. On 15 May 1898, Bierce notes that these men offer nothing more in their accounts and drawings than what De Forest and Keegan would call the standard battle-piece: "the rearing charger topped by a sword-waving general encouraging a corporal's guard" (qtd. in *Skepticism* 24). He asserts in his next column (22 May 1898) that the reason these writers and artists produce such unrevelatory work is that they lack the education necessary to understand what they are supposed to be reporting. Regarding correspondents who discuss "forts, guns and warships without having observed them, and battles without having seen one," Bierce says, "When a man writes on military matters without some degree of special training, study, and the technical knowledge so obtained, he makes a fool of himself in the first sentence, in the last and in all the intermediate sentences. No subject, not even art or literature, is beset with so many pitfalls for the confident ignoramus—the layman happy in unconsciousness of his own fallibility" (qtd. in *Skepticism* 35–36).

Still vexed two months later (31 July 1898) by the continuing inaccuracy of combat reporting, Bierce proposes a direct solution:

> Why not have a training school for war correspondents? Such an institution could turn out correspondents able to grasp the distinction between a redoubt and a battery of horse artillery and immune from the conviction, natural but erroneous, that an armistice is a place where they keep guns. Such knowledge as that would have a certain value to gentlemen writing from the seat of war to the seat of peace, and would be not altogether devoid of advantage to the civilian reader, in that it would insure him news that he could comprehend without taking off his coat and rolling up his sleeves. (Qtd. in *Skepticism* 89)

My earlier remarks about Bierce's assessment of all military history as untruthful notwithstanding, this proposal suggests that Bierce believes that accurate military history is at least theoretically possible, if rare in practice. Bierce does in fact feel this way; in several of his *Examiner* columns on the Spanish-American War he himself derives a usable meaning from history, drawing on the example of the Civil War as a whole to emphasize the necessity of military training to success in the field. Asserting on 1 May 1898 that the army's overall commander, General Nelson Miles, is not qualified to direct the impending conflict, Bierce points out that Miles "is a self-taught soldier, and military history in this country affords no instance of notable success of such in independent command. Among American generals all the conspicuously capable ones have been regularly educated to the difficult trade of war, at military institutions" (qtd. in *Skepticism* 10).

Responding on 19 February 1899 to President McKinley's and Secretary of War Alger's numerous appointments of politically influential but militarily inexperienced men to important army and navy commands, Bierce again invokes history, saying,

> The tremendous lessons of the civil war seem to have taught Messrs. McKinley and Alger nothing worth knowing. To observers of intelligence they taught one thing more thoroughly than anything else, namely, the incomparable advantage of a military education. Among all the scores of able civilians made into soldiers and put in command of large bodies of troops, not one accomplished anything notable in the conduct of an independent operation.... All the generals of just renown on both sides of that protracted conflict were graduates of the military academy at West Point. (Qtd. in *Skepticism* 150)

Thus far Bierce once again plainly sounds like De Forest, asserting as De Forest did in "Our Military Past and Future" that thorough training produces successful soldiers and that a combination of such training with firsthand observation can produce competent writers on military matters. Following De Forest's logic, we might assume that Bierce would therefore also find that successful soldiers are the best authors of useful military history. It is at this point, however, that Bierce and De Forest part company in their attitudes toward war literature. Although Bierce views the history of the Civil War as instructive as a whole, he sees an entirely accurate view of any of its specific battles as almost impossible, for if civilians are prevented from telling the truth by a lack of training, soldiers are equally hampered by their limitations of sight and understanding during an engagement, and in most cases, as might be inferred from his mention of "soldiers mostly fools" as writers of history in his *Devil's Dictionary* definition, by their desire to enhance or protect their own reputations afterward, which usually translates into a downplaying of those limitations and of the horrors of battle that might be regarded as having also blunted their personal effectiveness. Bierce makes frequent references to this desire throughout his war memoirs. In "What Occurred at Franklin," for instance, he asserts that the engagement of the title would likely have been a Confederate rather than a Union victory had the Confederates exploited a great tactical opportunity in the early stages of the battle. At this point, Bierce explains, one Union division lay isolated and exposed to Confederate attack. This force should have been annihilated, opening the way to a rout of the entire Union army, but the Confederates permitted it to escape without even being fired upon, for reasons that will never be clear because two Southern generals told different stories, each attempting to shift the fault for this blunder to the other. Bierce reports that John Bell Hood, the commander of the Confederate army, "declared that he gave the needful orders [for an attack on this division] and tried vainly to enforce them; [Benjamin] Cheatham, in command of [Hood's] leading corps, declared that he did not" (64). With both officers dead at the time he writes, Bierce wryly concludes, "[d]oubtless the dispute is still being carried on between these chieftains from their beds of asphodel and moly in Elysium" (64).[7]

In another piece, Bierce is less flippant about an instance of a general's claiming credit for a victory not rightly his, largely because in this case the general had no trouble dispelling the doubts that continued to cloud both Hood's and Cheatham's disclaimers of responsibility for the defeat at Franklin. In his *Examiner* column for 4 December 1898, he notes that the recent death of former Union general Don Carlos Buell has "provoked hardly a ripple of interest"; he accounts for this circumstance by explaining that thirty-six years earlier Ulysses Grant had refused to give Buell official credit for bringing his army to the rescue of Grant's shattered forces on the second day of the battle of Shiloh, because such an acknowledgment would have constituted an admission that on the first day Grant had been mentally unstrung by the Confederates' surprise attack and as a result had handled his army incompetently. In both his official reports at the time and later in his memoirs, Grant asserted that the Confederate assault had not caught him off guard, that he remained in full control of his faculties, and that, despite his army's demoralization and heavy losses on the first day of the battle, he would have rallied his troops and defeated the Confederates on the second day even had Buell not arrived. William T. Sherman, who served under Grant in this engagement, supported these contentions, but almost all other contemporary military analysts, including Buell, in his own official reports, and Bierce, who was in Buell's force, believed that Grant had indeed been caught unawares and rendered incapable. Their assessment was that at nightfall on the first day Grant's army was little more than a mob that the Confederates would have annihilated the next morning if Buell's divisions had not reached the scene overnight. Grant was relieved of command shortly after the battle, but, Bierce says, with Sherman's connivance he managed to shunt Buell's account aside and get his own report accepted as the official truth, thus writing a history in which he was the sole victor of Shiloh, an achievement that helped spark his rise to overall command of the Union armies and ultimately to the White House. Buell, on the other hand, stinging from this denial of rightful recognition, resigned from the army and faded into obscurity. By way of valediction, Bierce says, "if ever that turbulent time have a competent historian who had nothing to do with it the name of Don Carlos Buell will not need to be shouted in letters of brass to obtain an honorable renown" (qtd. in *Skepticism* 136).[8]

This mention of a competent, disinterested historian suggests once again that Bierce believes accurate military history is theoretically possible, a notion given further support by his statement that in the controversy over Buell's role at Shiloh Buell showed "literary qualities of the highest order" and demonstrated "immeasurable superiority" to Grant and Sherman "in clarity of mind and conscience" (qtd. in *Skepticism* 136). For Bierce, then, military skill can conceivably translate into literary truth. However, Bierce's opinion is also that such translations almost never actually occur, for these attributes have little to do with carving out a successful military career, and those men who do have successful military careers are the ones who ordinarily get to write the official histories.[9] Indeed, Bierce's handling of the example of Grant at Shiloh implies that writing falsehoods and military advancement have a direct relationship, in a logic-circumventing crossruff that would not be out of place in Joseph Heller's *Catch-22*. A general falsely claims credit for a victory actually won through the good judgment of a subordinate or through the simple fortunate coincidences of the battlefield. This claim establishes him, in the eyes of his superiors and the public, as a successful soldier. Therefore, because—as in De Forest's formulation—successful soldiers are reputed to tell the truth about battles, the claim manages to confirm itself, despite contradictory reports from other witnesses: General X writes that he won the battle, which makes him a good soldier; good soldiers do not lie, so he must have won the battle.

In Bierce's view, then, successful soldiers are not those possessed of great military minds but those most adept at claiming credit for others' achievements and evading responsibility for their own mistakes. The most skillful soldier he ever knew, Bierce says in "The Crime at Pickett's Mill," was his then-brigade commander, General William Hazen. But Hazen's career was troubled, Bierce continues, because Hazen was dedicated to telling the truth, even when doing so meant attempting to hold his superiors, including Grant, Sherman, and Sheridan, accountable for their errors. As a result, Hazen constantly faced courts-martial and courts of inquiry on various trumped-up charges; such were his superiors' methods of protecting themselves (41).

Bierce's view of most military history, therefore, is that, because it is written by successful soldiers, who to have become successful necessarily lack the "clarity of mind and conscience" of a Buell or a Hazen, it is largely made up of outright lies, selective omissions, and, at best, statements that take full advantage of the ability of military language to drain the unfortunate character from what it describes without actually falsifying the event. Regarding straightforward lying, Bierce notes in a short story, "The Coup de Grâce," that after a battle Union troopers make an effort to identify their own dead but that "[t]he enemy's fallen had to be content with counting. But of that they got enough: many of them were counted several times, and the total, as given afterward in the official report of the victorious commander, denoted rather a hope than a result" (154). Regarding military language's more subtle powers of obscurantism, Bierce recalls in a memoir, "A Bivouac of the Dead," that one of the first engagements he ever witnessed, a Union brigade's vain attempt to take a Confederate position by assault, was officially listed in the Union commander's reports as a "reconnaissance in force" (71)—a substitution of successful semantics for failed tactics.

Bierce makes similar passing references to history's inadequacy in most of his war writings, but two pieces, the memoir "The Crime at Pickett's Mill" and the short story "Jupiter Doke, Brigadier-General," do more; from start to finish Bierce's purpose in these accounts is a clear and systematic indictment of military history as it is usually written. Bierce intends in "Pickett's Mill" to tell the truth about a little-known and poorly understood engagement in which he participated, but in doing so he emphasizes the difficulty of that task and thus calls into question the veracity of other writers who suggest that the process of reconstructing a battle is a simple matter. History's usual unreliability as a result of its being the creation of self-interested reporters is the very first note this account strikes; Bierce begins by saying that the battle of Pickett's Mill is one of a "class of events which by their very nature, and despite any intrinsic interest that they may possess, are foredoomed to oblivion" (38)—the result of such events' being injurious to the reputations of those involved whose duty it is to report them. Pickett's Mill was a Union defeat, Bierce says, and therefore only "imperfect accounts" of it exist, because "the vanquished have not thought it expedient to relate it. It is ignored by General Sherman in his memoirs, yet Sherman ordered it. General Howard wrote an account of the campaign of which it was an incident, and dismissed it in a single sentence; yet General Howard planned it, and it was fought as an isolated and independent action under his eye" (38).

Bierce asserts that his purpose is to reveal what he regards as Howard's criminal lack of military judgment in this battle by showing, as Howard neglects to point out in his one-sentence account of it, that the general pointlessly ordered a single brigade to assault four times their number of Confederates dug in behind well-fortified entrenchments.[10] In describing this event, however, Bierce almost immediately runs into his own problem with telling the truth. After detailing the location and disposition of both armies at the time of the Union attack, he says, as noted earlier in this chapter, "The civilian reader must not suppose when he reads accounts of military operations in which relative position[s] of the forces are defined . . . that these were matters of general knowledge to those engaged. . . . It is seldom, indeed, that a subordinate officer [i.e., Bierce himself] knows anything about the disposition of the enemy's forces . . . or precisely whom he is fighting" (39).[11]

For Bierce to purport to present his indictment of Howard entirely as an eyewitness account, then, would be a falsification of the same type generals and other memoirists engage in when they neglect to mention the fact emphasized in the above statement—that they are writing from a perspective gained after the encounter rather than one they possessed during it. Through this omission, they impose a single, unified, omniscient narrative perspective on their material, which enhances their own military acuity by suggesting that they acted during the battle on knowledge that they did not possess until afterward—by suggesting, in other words, that they found battle far more manageable intellectually than was actually the case.

This presentation of events through only one narrative viewpoint is standard practice in military history. For an example we have only to recall "The First Time Under Fire." Although De Forest later admitted to Howells that "nothing is more confounding, fragmentary, incomprehensible than a battle as one sees it" (qtd. in *Adventures* 204), in this account he nonetheless shifts back and forth from descriptions of his own sights and actions to the larger tactical and strategic picture, as contained in the official reports of the battle written after the fact,[12] with no break in his narrative voice or consciousness, no indication that he derives these separate visions from separate sources. To draw a cinematic analogy, De Forest gives the impression that he and the reader look through a single camera fitted with a zoom lens capable of effortless movements from extreme closeup to extreme long shot. But for Bierce this standard approach is entirely false, for it fails to capture what happened—what any individual participant actually saw, did, and felt—at the time of the battle. Instead, it filters events through later knowledge without a clear admission of that process.

This insight is of course not original with Bierce, having been a part of war literature since the inception of the genre in the *Iliad,* in which Homer says in book 12, "Now there was fighting at the various gates— / a difficult thing for me to tell it all / as though I were a god" (286). Bierce is not even the first Civil War writer to raise it, since, as Timothy Sweet points out, Walt Whitman in *Specimen Days* provides many detailed descriptions of battles in which the ultimate point is that such descriptions are fragmentary. For Whitman, Sweet says, "the 'realistic' description is always fragmentary, and framed by claims . . . which question the possibility of representation and suggest that 'the real war will never get in the books.' The vivid details function, paradoxically, to indicate a lack of adequate detail" (49). On this subject, as Sweet notes, Whitman himself says, as early as 1863, "We already talk of Histories of the War, (presently to accumulate)—yes—technical histories of some things, statistics, official reports, and so on—but shall we ever get histories of the *real* things? . . . What history, I say, can ever give—for who can know—the mad determin'd tussle of the armies, in all their separate large and little squads . . . each steeped from crown to toe in desperate, mortal purports?" (*Specimen Days* 54).

Nevertheless, at the time Bierce is writing, Homer and Whitman notwithstanding, the official records of Sherman and Howard, among others, have been accepted as giving the histories of the real things, and Bierce wants his reader to remain aware that the genuine truth is more complicated—and, as is implicit in the Whitman passage as well, more horrifying—than their "single-camera" approach suggests. He wants his reader to remain aware, as G. Thomas Couser says, that "the official discourse misled not only by means of its selective contents but also by means of its distanced, retrospective narrative, the Olympian perspective of which effaced the chaos, confusion, and carnage of war" (92).[13] In Bierce's view, the truth, in all its chaos, confusion, and carnage, comes from many separate and frequently contradictory accounts that can only be provisionally pieced together, and anyone who claims to be able to present a battle as a seamlessly meaningful whole is to be distrusted as having a personal motive to advance. To give a truly accurate account of the battle by his own definition of accuracy—emphasizing discontinuity and a range of separate, limited visions—Bierce employs multiple narrative perspectives throughout his memoir, expressly calling the reader's attention to his shifts from what he himself witnessed to what he learned from other reports.

Bierce makes clear early on, for instance, that he himself did not hear Howard issue the fateful order but instead learned of it from Hazen, his brigade commander. He says he takes Hazen's word that this order was in fact given, however, because of Hazen's lifelong devotion to telling the truth, especially with regard to his superior officers' failings (40–41). After this explanation, Bierce turns to a description of the position his brigade is about to attack, but rather than simply detailing it in his own words, as though he perfectly understood this entrenchment at the time, he reminds the reader that he is piecing together the facts long after the event by quoting directly from the reports of Confederate Generals Johnston and Hood, who were in overall and immediate command of this position, respectively. Moreover, he further emphasizes the complexity of truth by pointing out a mistake in Johnston's account, noting that Johnston claims that the attack proceeded from a line of Union entrenchments whereas he himself, as an eyewitness on the Union side, knows that this line was not entrenched (42). Once again, Bierce's point is that no one report can tell the whole truth: while Bierce himself does not pretend to certainty regarding the Confederate position because he did not see it, Johnston's misapprehension reveals the inadequacy of such a pretense.

Bierce continues this shifting of perspectives, cross-checking one against the other for veracity in order to get at as much of the whole truth as possible, throughout the memoir. After describing the chaotic nature of the attack itself, which he witnessed firsthand and which is quoted earlier in this chapter, he returns to Johnston's report. This time, however, his demonstration of the complexities of arriving at the truth is more intricate than previously, for here he shows that even some misunderstandings of events on various witnesses' parts may be integral elements of a larger truth when they are viewed in the light of other accounts. Seeking to confirm his brigade's valor in this encounter as proof that the assault failed because Howard sent in too few troops rather than because the attackers lacked resolution, Bierce quotes from Johnston's report. Johnston says, "'The [Union] Fourth Corps came on in deep order and assailed [the Confederates] with great vigor, receiving their close and accurate fire with the fortitude always exhibited by General Sherman's troops in the actions of this campaign'" (45).

This statement is another misapprehension on Johnston's part, Bierce says, for it was not the entire Fourth Corps but only one brigade—approximately a quarter of the Fourth Corps—that made this assault.[14] But, he continues, this report, false on the simplest level of fact, actually reveals the deeper truth of the brigade's valor, since "nothing could more truly indicate the resolute nature of the attack than the Confederate belief that it was made by the whole Fourth Corps, instead of one weak brigade" (44–45).

Further confirmation of the brigade's courage comes later in Johnston's account, this time in a passage Bierce himself can verify. Bierce quotes Johnston's recollection that "'[w]hen the United States troops paused in their advance within fifteen paces of the [Confederate] front rank, one of their color-bearers planted his colors eight or ten feet in front of his regiment, and was instantly shot dead. A soldier sprang forward to his place and fell also as he grasped the color-staff. A second and third followed successively, and each received death as speedily as his predecessors. A fourth, however, seized and bore back the object of soldierly devotion'" (45).

Regarding this incident of heroism, Bierce continues, "I can attest the truth of [Johnston's] soldierly praise: I saw the occurrence that he relates and regret that I am unable to recall even the name of the regiment whose colors were so gallantly saved" (45). Again, Bierce's underlying point is that one can only recover any truth about a battle by careful and frankly acknowledged cross-referencing and -verification of several accounts. A corollary of this point also presents itself in Bierce's last sentence: although one may discover some of the truth through this process of cross-checking, the whole truth can never be reconstructed, for even all the reporters together do not know everything—such as the identity of the regiment in question in this case.[15]

Having made his point about the inadequacy of military history as customarily written, Bierce drives home his message by concluding this memoir as he began, emphasizing the contradictions found in separate sources and the impossibility as a result of ever recovering the whole truth. Bierce notes that General Hazen's account of the engagement sets the Union casualties at fourteen hundred, while Johnston's report says that the Confederates counted seven hundred Union killed and wounded. "This is obviously erroneous," Bierce says of Johnston's claim, but because he himself "[has] not the means at hand to ascertain the true number," the best he can honestly do is give his impressions: "I remember that we were all astonished at the uncommonly large proportion of dead to wounded—a consequence of the uncommonly close range at which most of the fighting was done" (49).[16] Bierce has recovered the central facts Howard and Sherman ignore, that the brigade fought well and was undone by Howard's tactical incompetence, but the memoir nevertheless ends on this note of ambiguity regarding the limits of even the best history—the best precisely because of those limits, because its writer is completely forthright about its being pieced together from various incomplete and contradictory reports.

In one respect, however, Bierce is not entirely forthright. Although the impression he wishes to give in this piece is that he has sifted through various accounts to arrive at a synthesis that approaches the truth, the actuality of its composition, as Napier Wilt demonstrates in a seminal article on Bierce's Civil War memoirs, is that he derived all of his various perspectives from only one source outside his own recollections, General Hazen's *Narrative of Military Service*. Wilt points out that although the quotations from Johnston's and Hood's accounts give the impression that Bierce himself combed through the *Official Records,* all the passages Bierce cites from these accounts are also quoted in Hazen's narrative (270). That Bierce was conversant with Hazen's work is borne out, Wilt continues, by the similarities between Bierce's introduction to his account of Pickett's Mill and Hazen's opening paragraphs regarding this engagement. Both writers deplore the battle's unjustifiably sketchy treatment in Sherman's and Howard's reports and memoirs and say that they intend their accounts to give this fight its proper place in Civil War history (280).[17] It would seem that here, in his omission of the reality of his compositional process, in his downplaying of his deriving his various perspectives from only one source, Bierce unintentionally offers two insights: he reveals his own sacrifice of a certain degree of "fact" in order to highlight his "truth," and he also reveals that Hazen, in his prior attacks on the omissions endemic to "official" history and his use of multiple perspectives to recover these omissions and point up the impossibility of ever recovering the full truth, was the one military writer who seems unquestionably to have positively influenced him.

An event that proved deeply ironic in light of both Hazen's and Bierce's account of Pickett's Mill (which first appeared in the *Examiner* for 27 May 1888) prompted Bierce to express even more vehemently his feelings about history's inadequacies. In 1894 no less a "historian" than the selective General Howard was named editor of the *Magazine of American History.* In the *Examiner* for 11 October of that year, Bierce observes that with Howard in charge, once again history will not serve the truth. "General Howard's hardihood in accentuating his connection with American history," Bierce says,

> transcends the limits of human effrontery and passes into the circumcluding domain of infinite gall. This military Quaker, spirited sheeply and skilled in the tactics of confusion and the strategy of retreat, will . . . try to keep with his pen the place in American history that he won with his heels. . . .
>
> I once had the honor to serve as a staff officer under this consummate master of the art of needless defeat, and [at Pickett's Mill]

he made the critical Confederate eye familiar with my back—which is not handsome. I said then that I would get even if spared, and . . . these remarks are in part performance of that pious vow. . . .

Down in Georgia is a little forest [Pickett's Mill] where the blood of six hundred of my fifteen hundred battlemates utters a mute demand for recognition and place in this revenge. It took them only twenty minutes to fall, but it has taken General Howard thirty years to ignore their hopeless heroism, and he has not finished. He was probably the only officer present who expected a different result; but . . . I am bound to confess that he has borne his disappointment with a more unfailing cheerfulness than the rest of us have felt in the memory of our fulfilled expectations. *Vale,* General Howard!—may you live forever! And may every unctuous smile of your life cover a warm and comfortable consciousness of your soldierly generosity in enriching American history with *one line* about the affair at Pickett's Mill. (Qtd. in *Skepticism* 118)

Hazen's and Bierce's accounts, telling as much of the truth as can be honestly recovered, are ignored; Howard's version, because of its very dishonesty, is hailed as the work of a successful soldier and enshrined as history. In fulminating against this state of affairs, Bierce seems to anticipate Paul de Man's dictum that "the bases for historical knowledge are not empirical facts but written texts, even if these masquerade in the guise of wars or revolutions" (165), and perhaps also Fredric Jameson's assertion that "history is not a text, not a narrative, master or otherwise, but . . . an absent cause . . . inaccessible to us except in textual form" (35). In light of these statements, Bierce can be understood as seeking, in both the content and the multiple-perspective form of his memoirs, to enlighten readers who mistake texts such as Howard's for the war itself, and, in supplanting these univocal texts with his own polyphonic ones, to make sure those readers recognize the limitations of accessibility to history inherent in any text.

What Bierce does not explain in his attacks on Grant, Sherman, and Howard, nor indeed directly in any of his memoirs or stories, is *how* such generals are able to keep with their pens their places in American history—how they get their accounts of battles accepted as the truth despite more powerfully written competing discourses such as Buell's and Bierce's own reports of Shiloh and Hazen's and Bierce's of Pickett's Mill. Several recent historiographical works, however, do provide a possible answer. In *The Content of the Form,* a study of narrative discourse in historical writing, Hayden White asserts that ordinarily a specific version of events finds its place in a historical narrative, with the narrative form in turn confirming this version's "reality," because it "conduce[s] to the establishment of social order" (23). In wartime, nothing is more conducive to establishing and maintaining social order than the belief that a general is a capable, inspiring leader—that he is, in fact, a hero. Therefore, the majority is always more inclined to accept as true a discourse that reinforces this belief than one that shows a commander to be less than a great leader of men. As shown by Alan T. Nolan in *Lee Considered,* a study of the rapid accretion of heroic myths around Robert E. Lee, and by Charles Royster in *The Destructive War,* a similar examination of the celebrity of Sherman and Stonewall Jackson,[18] the Civil War was no exception to this principle; in order to continue prosecuting the war the populace needed a belief in the absolute, unwavering heroism of its armies' leaders—what Simon Schama, regarding another general in another war, calls "the grandiloquent lie the public crave[s]" (30).[19] Thus, in the case of Grant at Shiloh, for example, Northern readers in general—and, crucially, the politicians, senior army officers, and newspaper editors whose interests lay in stoking those readers' continued enthusiasm for the war—were all more than willing to privilege Grant's own account of the battle's events, constructing an image of himself as imperturbable in momentary setbacks and able to win through to final victory by his implacable determination, over another version that revealed him to be dangerously susceptible to breakdown under the pressures of combat command.

Evidence that Bierce sees this particular interaction between reader and writer as the key to the success of Grant's, Sherman's, and Howard's lies is found in "Jupiter Doke, Brigadier-General." This short story can be read as a wilder, fictionalized companion-piece to "The Crime at Pickett's Mill," since, like that memoir, it focuses on the contradictions among multiple accounts of the same military occurrences, but it does so in an absurdist, blackly humorous vein that has led Cathy Davidson to call it a spiritual if not indeed literal ancestor of *Catch-22* (72). Probably based on an actual incident in the Union army of the Cumberland's campaign to capture

Chattanooga, in which Bierce participated,[20] the story is essentially epistolary, being structured as a collection of letters and other sorts of statements from eight people regarding the same events, the significant moments in the career of Union general Jupiter Doke. Through the separate levels of knowledge and differences in intent on the parts of various characters that these competing discourses enable him to reveal, Bierce once again emphasizes the difficulty of recovering the whole truth, particularly when military men are determined to make that truth appear as advantageous as possible to themselves. Anticipating White, Nolan, Royster, and Schama, the story charts the rise of an officer whose pusillanimity on the battlefield is more than offset by his understanding that the public will readily accept any lies he chooses to tell about his combat achievements as long as he casts himself as a hero in those lies.

The story's first section is a series of letters from Doke, Doke's commanding officer, Major-General Blount Wardorg, and the secretary of war to one another. These letters reveal various levels of truth in various individuals' possession, with no one knowing everything. The secretary sets the story's action in motion by offering Doke a commission as brigadier-general of volunteers. Doke's florid acceptance, consisting chiefly of a pledge that "the patronage of my office will be bestowed with an eye single to securing the greatest good to the greatest number, the stability of republican institutions, and the triumph of the party in all elections" (247), makes it clear that he has attained this position of military eminence not because of any martial experience in his past but because of his political power in his home county in Illinois. His subsequent statements also make clear that his ideas of service to his country are limited to using his rank to make speeches that will enhance his political standing and to secure government contracts for his supporters and relatives. Meanwhile, the correspondence between the secretary and General Wardorg, which Bierce intersperses with that between Doke and the secretary, reveals that more is going on than Doke has been told. The secretary orders Doke to join Wardorg's command by traveling in full uniform through country heavily infested with Confederate guerrillas; his plan, as he explains to Wardorg, is that the militarily worthless Doke will be killed or captured and the guerillas will thereby reveal their positions, enabling Wardorg to clear them out. What the secretary does not know, however, is that this area is currently flooded; as a result, Doke, unaware of the sacrificial role he is supposed to play, journeys safely by steamboat to Wardorg's camp.

The story's second section continues this discrepancy between what Doke understands and what the secretary and Wardorg intend, but it also adds another layer of intentional misunderstanding, this one promulgated by Doke himself. In his diary Doke honestly describes his first experience of combat—a comic-opera fiasco—and his own terrified response to it. Notified that an artillery battery is on its way to join his brigade, Doke marches his command out of its camp at Distilleryville, Kentucky, to meet the new arrivals at Jayhawk, three miles to the rear, but

> their chairman, mistaking us for the opposing party [revealing that only one frame of reference and its particular form of discourse have significance for him, Doke consistently describes his military experiences in political terms], opened fire on the head of the procession and by the extraordinary noise of the cannon balls (I had no conception of it!) so frightened my horse that I was unseated without a contest. The meeting adjourned in disorder and returning to camp I found that a deputation of the enemy had crossed the river in our absence and made a division of the loaves and fishes. (252)

Doke's initial response to this experience, which he evidently found still more frightening than did his horse, given his parenthetical exclamation, is to attempt an escape; "Wrote to the President, applying for the Gubernatorial Chair of the Territory of Idaho" is the final sentence of this "combat" account (252). But a more rewarding course of action quickly suggests itself, as the story's next entry, an editorial from Doke's home-county newspaper, the Posey *Maverick,* reveals. This passage indicates that Doke has offered for public consumption a much different version of his first "battle," one that makes no mention of the terrors of finding himself under fire for the first time and his consequent inability to command his horse, his troops, or himself. The paper's editor proudly declares that

> Brigadier-General Doke's thrilling account, in another column, of the Battle of Distilleryville will make the heart of every loyal Illinoisian leap with exultation. . . . [H]is account of the strategic ruse by which

> he apparently abandoned his camp and so inveigled a perfidious enemy into it for the purpose of murdering the sick, the unfortunate *countertempus* at Jayhawk, the subsequent dash upon a trapped enemy flushed with a supposed success, driving their terrified legions across an impassable river which precluded pursuit—all these "moving accidents by flood and field" are related with a pen of fire and have all the terrible interest of romance. (252–53)

Doke's account might as well have "all the terrible interest of romance," since it clearly has nothing to do with reality. What it *does* have to do with is his readers' overriding desire to see Doke as a hero and the editor's self-serving, sales-boosting willingness to satisfy that desire, both of which are evidenced most blatantly in the editor's cynical inclusion of Doke's claim about the enemy's escape over an "impassable" river.[21] Despite such patent absurdities, Doke's construction of himself as a leader unruffled in combat effectively conduces to social order and thus guarantees the acceptance of his account as the truth. The editor follows the passage quoted above by exclaiming, "Verily, truth is stranger than fiction and the pen is mightier than the sword" (253). The editor's readers miss the irony here, but Bierce's reader does not. Instead, he or she recognizes the heart of the problem in the editor's ensuing expression of delight at having been able to acquire "the services of so distinguished a contributor as the Great Captain who made the history as well as wrote it" (253). The editor intends for his readers to discern some level of separation between making history and writing it, but Bierce's reader grasps the full meaning of the claim that the pen is mightier than the sword, for Doke here demonstrates that history is literally *made* with the pen, not the sword.[22]

The rest of the story further bears out the problems inherent in entrusting the writing of history to the same people who supposedly make it, for in reporting his next battle Doke demonstrates that not only can he get accounts of his own heroism accepted despite their clear spuriousness when, as in the preceding case, they are evidently the sole accounts available, but also that, like Grant's report of Shiloh, his version will carry the field simply by virtue of its heroic tenor even when it faces specific competing discourses. Frustrated by the incompetence Doke demonstrated at Distilleryville, the secretary of war and General Wardorg formulate a second plan to sacrifice him. Notified that the Confederates have massed twenty thousand troops just across the river from his command, Wardorg, with the secretary's approval, posts only Doke's brigade to guard against their crossing, hoping the Rebel army will take full advantage of its superior numbers. Once again, however, the plan goes awry. Doke, having had enough of battle at Distilleryville, informs Wardorg that he has removed his headquarters to the rear, explaining that his purpose is "to point the way whenever my brigade retires" (254), and that he has commandeered twenty-three hundred mules to facilitate his troops' anticipated retreat. What happens subsequently varies widely in the ensuing reports from the generals involved. Bierce's next entry is a letter from the Confederates' Major-General Gibeon Buxter to the Confederate secretary of war. Buxter explains that two divisions, his own and one commanded by Major-General Dolliver Billows, crossed the river with the intention of destroying Doke's brigade[23] and then advancing against the Federal main body, but they were nearly annihilated by "one of the terrible tornadoes for which this region is famous" (256), in the course of which General Billows was killed.

Billows, however, is not dead, for he weighs in with a different report immediately following Buxter's. His own division is intact, Billows explains, but Buxter's is destroyed and Buxter is dead, having been taken by surprise by fifty thousand Union cavalry who had learned of the Confederates' approach from a spy and secretly reinforced the single Union infantry brigade guarding the crossing (256–57). A more honest if no more revelatory account comes from a third Confederate source, Brigadier-General Schneddeker Baumschank, who commanded the force's artillery. Baumschank had just crossed the river, he explains, when "somdings occur, I know nod vot it vas—somdings mackneefcent, but it vas nod vor—und I finds meinselluf, afder leedle viles, in dis blace, midout a horse und mit no men und goons" (257).

That Doke offers still another version of what that "somdings" was, neither tornado nor cavalry, is apparent in the next entry, a resolution of Congress recommending Doke's promotion to major-general and thanking his brigade for their "unparalleled feat of attacking—themselves only 2000 strong—an army of 25,000 men and utterly overthrowing it" (257). As Doke pins on his second star, Bierce concludes the story with the statement of another witness who, since he is not a general and thus has no stake in these events,[24] may be more readily trusted than Billows, Buxter, or Doke to explain what actually happened. In the words of Doke's African American servant, Hannibal Peyton,

> Dat wus a almighty dark night, sho', and dese yere ole eyes aint wuf shuks, but I's got a year like a sque'l, an' w'en I cotch de mummer o' v'ices I knowed dat gang b'long on de far side o' de ribber. So I jes' runs in de house an' wakes Marse Doke an' tells him: "Skin outer dis fo' yo' life!" An' de Lo'd bress my soul! ef dat man didn' go right fru de winder in his shir' tail an' break for to cross de mule patch! An' dem twenty-free hunerd mules dey jes' t'ink it is de debble hese'f wid de brandin' iron, an' dey bu'st outen dat patch like a yarthquake, an' pile inter de upper ford road, an' flash down it five deep, an' it full o' Confed'rates from en' to en'! . . . (258)

The fact is, then, that the Confederates were routed by a mule stampede set off by the terrified Doke himself, which this general has written into a fearless attack by his brigade, presumably with himself at its head. (Another presumption we may make, noting the discrepancy between the twenty thousand Confederates reported to Wardorg and the twenty-five thousand appearing in the congressional resolution, is that Doke in his report has inflated his foe's numbers by 25 percent, doubtless to add a finishing touch of grandiloquence to his lie.) The reality of these events is at least initially recoverable, Bierce implies, by including Peyton's narrative, but since this account lacks a heroic leader, as do Buxter's, Billows's, and Baumschank's, it like them has no place in the official accounts; instead, Doke continues his military rise thanks to the public's readiness to give credence to his literary construction of himself as a paragon of coolness under fire and in the face of impossible odds. If, as Scarry argues, the dead or wounded body of a soldier—any casualty of war—is "a referentially unstable sign that is appropriated by the discourse of the war to legitimate the ideology of the victor state" (117), then Doke's success demonstrates that this dictum applies as well regarding the truth, since it, in Hiram Johnson's famous description, is the first casualty of war.[25]

Given history's unreliability as revealed in "Pickett's Mill" and "Jupiter Doke," it is not surprising that a number of Bierce's stories focus on the disillusionment, or worse, of a civilian who approaches battle with a set of expectations derived from history or the historical rituals through which an army sustains itself. In "An Affair of Outposts" the governor of an unnamed Northern state visits the front lines during the Union army's campaign to capture Corinth, Mississippi, following the battle of Shiloh. Finding himself unexpectedly in the middle of a skirmish in a forest, he is initially terrified by his inability to see the Confederates whose Minié balls are whizzing all around him. His abhorrence grows still stronger when he begins to focus on what he can see: first, wounded Union men stumbling toward safety, and then their unhurt comrades, who struggle past him singly and by twos in retreat, occasionally pausing to turn and fire at the unseen enemy but not stopping to help the injured. "In all this," the narrator reports the governor as thinking,

> was none of the pomp of war—no hint of glory. Even in his distress and peril the helpless civilian could not forbear to contrast it with the gorgeous parades and reviews held in honor of himself—with the brilliant uniforms, the music, the banners, and the marching. It was an ugly and sickening business. . . .
> "Ugh!" he grunted, shuddering—"this is beastly! Where is the charm of it all? Where are the elevated sentiments, the devotion, the heroism. . . ." (179)

Bierce's two best-known war stories likewise conform to this pattern of disillusionment regarding war's relationship to history. In "An Occurrence at Owl Creek Bridge," the aristocratic Southern civilian Peyton Farquhar has high expectations of military service; he is "longing for the release of his energies, the larger life of the soldier, the opportunity for distinction" (89). Thus, he is easily recruited as a saboteur, with the task of blowing up a bridge to deny its use to the Union forces in the region, by a man whom he believes to be a Confederate soldier but who is in fact a Union spy. What he discovers as a result is that war is a squalid business, in which the enemy will disguise himself to lure a man to his doom, and in which one is more likely to die ingloriously swinging from a railroad bridge than while leading a triumphant cavalry charge.[26]

Equally squalid discoveries obtain in "Chickamauga," for the deaf-mute child protagonist ends up inarticulately gabbling his sense of horror at the discovery that war has destroyed his home and shattered his mother's skull. And here the inadequacy of history as a preparation for an individual experience of battle is even more overt, since Bierce explicitly presents this boy as a product of the historical continuum of war. The first thing the reader learns about this child is that his "spirit, in the bodies of its ancestors, had for thousands of years been trained to memorable feats of discovery and conquest—victories in battles whose critical moments were centuries, whose victors' camps were cities of hewn stone. From the cradle of its race it had conquered its way through two continents and passing a great sea had penetrated a third, there to be born to war and dominion as a heritage" (99). The narrator says, moreover, that this boy's father had himself been a soldier in the Mexican War and "loved military books and pictures" (99), from which the boy has acquired his enthusiasm for playing soldier.

Despite the martial heritage of both his race and his father's library, however, the child does not recognize actual war when he encounters it. Representations of casualties evidently had no place in his father's military books and pictures, for when the boy sees the wounded men of Chickamauga dragging themselves toward the river, they do not look to him like what they are. Instead, they look first like babies, because of their crawling posture, then like circus clowns, because "[a]ll their faces were singularly white and many were streaked and gouted with red" (102), and finally, in one case, like a great bird of prey, because the man's lower jaw has been shot away. Only when the child finds his burning home and dead mother does he comprehend the true nature of war, its reasonless, arbitrary dealing of death and destruction. If history did not prepare him for the countenances of the wounded, neither did it ready him for this sight, in which he learns, in Lawrence Berkove's words, "the awesome role Chance play[s] in war, and the diminutive role of human intelligence" ("Arms" 25).

It is the omission of this last insight that Bierce believes is the greatest failure of history as written by men like Grant, Howard, and Jupiter Doke. Such men, in their determination to present themselves as the rational controllers of events, refuse to acknowledge that in reality those events are by their very nature so "beset with accident and dependent upon the unknowable and incalculable," as Bierce says (*Collected Works* 9: 305, qtd. in

Brazil 233), that they deny the "rational continuity of experience" (Ziff 172). In Bierce's view, the individual's apprehension of war is inevitably a discovery of irrationality and unknowability that drives that man into isolation and subjectivity. Therefore, for Bierce the only realistic combat writing is that which simply acknowledges these facts rather than trying to counteract them by suggesting that one can place them in an intelligible historical framework and thus rationally assimilate them. Once again, a comparison of Bierce's work to De Forest's will make this point clear.

In *Miss Ravenel's Conversion,* De Forest, drawing closely from his own experience as reported in *A Volunteer's Adventures,* places Colburne in a situation fraught with the irrational and unknowable during the assault on Port Hudson: Colburne is alone with his company in the forest, having no idea where the rest of his army is, not knowing the enemy's location, not even aware of whether he is to attack or defend. In this situation Colburne relies for guidance on the historical precedents encapsulated in the Army Regulations and thus is able to keep himself and his men from collapsing into individual reactions of panic. By contrast, Bierce describes himself in a similar situation in "What I Saw of Shiloh" as giving way to alienation and subjectivity as a result of his lack of understanding of his position. Unlike De Forest, who at the outset of all his combat descriptions, as in "The First Time Under Fire," takes care to explain the generals' plans and the armies' positions that led to the engagement, Bierce begins his account of Shiloh in medias res, with the Union army's troopers drowsing in their encampment on a Sunday morning when they suddenly hear cannon fire and realize they are under attack.[27] Through this strategy he emphasizes to the reader that, as he said in "Pickett's Mill," soldiers involved in a battle do not have the sort of context with which De Forest in his memoirs provides his reader, that instead they are suddenly confronted with events of which they have very little understanding. Moving to his own activities during the battle, Bierce explains that he himself has no more grasp of where he is or what he is supposed to be doing than does the army as a whole as he has just described it, or than Captain Colburne does at Port Hudson. He knows that his division is a part of Buell's force coming to Grant's army's rescue, but beyond that fact he is completely at a loss. "A few inaudible commands from an invisible leader had placed us in order of battle," Bierce says, establishing the note of incomprehension, "[b]ut where was the enemy? Where, too, were the riddled regiments that we had come to save? Had our other divisions arrived during the night and passed the river to assist us? Or were we to oppose our paltry five thousand breasts to an army flushed with victory? What protected our right? Who lay upon our left? Was there really anything in our front?" (19).

Not privy to the larger perspective that would provide answers to these questions, Bierce does not think to orient himself, as De Forest has Colburne do, by placing his immediate lack of knowledge in the still broader context of military history and Army Regulations, by reminding himself of his prescribed responsibilities in any such situation.[28] Instead, Bierce falls completely into alienation, dissociating himself from his men and the wounded Federal sergeant with the bitter joke already discussed and further emphasizing his isolation in subjectivity by employing figurative language to give the reader a picture not so much of what things actually look like as of what they look like to him, a technique that offers yet another illustration of the differences between Bierce's and De Forest's ideas about the nature of truth in combat writing. There is comparatively little figurative language in De Forest's descriptions of battles; De Forest concentrates on presenting what he or his protagonist sees and does on the battlefield in terms that accord with what anyone in this position would observe, a theoretically unmediated approach consistent with his criticism of the "billows of cavalry" school of combat writing. A typical description is this scene in "The First Time Under Fire," in which everything looks simply like what it is: "We were just entering a large open field, dotted by a few trees and thorn-bushes, with a swampy forest on the right and the levee of the bayou on the left, when the rebels gave us their musketry" (479). When De Forest resorts to an occasional simile or metaphor, what he regards as objective clarity is equally his primary goal; his purpose is to put a sight or sound that may be unfamiliar to a reader into terms that he or she may grasp more readily, with the added benefit that the homespun nature of this familiar imagery tends to domesticate the experience for the reader, making combat still more easily assimilable. To convey the noise of the Confederates' firing, he explains that "it was a long rattle like that which a boy makes in running with a stick along a picket fence, only vastly louder" (479). Similarly, the Confederates fleeing their defensive line in the face of De Forest's charging regiment scramble over one another in a movement that looks like that of "an immense flock of sheep swarming over a fence" (480). The implication of this style, focused on providing as precise and familiar a vision as possible, is that De Forest feels that by getting the surface details down accurately he, like the combat writers he admires, is conveying the truth about battle—that this experience can be rationally assimilated, recalled, and explained in concrete detail to a reader.

Bierce's description of Shiloh, by contrast, is suffused with imagery designed not to give the reader a clear, coherent, and essentially calming idea of what actually occurred but rather to illustrate the surreal dimensions the battle's sights and sounds assumed in Bierce's mind. In his description of the sound of enemy firing, Bierce begins with the same onomatopoeia as De Forest, *rattle,* but he follows it with the subjectivity of heavy personification: "To the right and the left the musketry rattled smartly and petulantly; directly in front it sighed and growled" (15). His descriptions of the combatants are often impressionistic as well. As night falls, ending the first day's fighting, Bierce notes that "occasionally, against the glare behind the trees, could be seen moving black figures, singularly distinct but apparently no longer than a thumb. They seemed to me ludicrously like the demons in old allegorical prints of hell" (15). With this hallucinatory mixture of terror and irony in mind, we do well to remember that this piece is titled "What *I* Saw of Shiloh"; in devoting most of his energies to describing not what the battle really looked like but rather the impressions his imagination generated from it at the time, Bierce suggests that the truth about combat has little to do with surface details or historical perspectives but is instead chiefly a matter of the individual's unavoidably subjective responses to it. The single objective truth in Bierce's battle writing is that any truth in it is subjective. To forget this fact, to believe that one can behave objectively in battle by relying on history to impose a rational perspective, is for Bierce the surest path to destruction, as illustrated in the two stories I will examine at some length in the next chapter.

CHAPTER 7

To March toward the Sound of the Guns

The memoirs covered in the previous chapter focus on Bierce's own experiences in the moment of battle, but none of the short stories considered thus far concerns itself with the reactions of its characters to this moment. Instead, they depict what happens to an individual at the edge of a battle zone, as in "An Occurrence at Owl Creek Bridge," or in the aftermath of a battle, treating such events comically in "Jupiter Doke" and tragically in "Chickamauga." Bierce casts most of his war stories in one of these molds; he ordinarily concentrates not on what transpires during an engagement but on the stresses an isolated protagonist feels before or after battle, stresses that drive such a character to desperate and often tragically ironic actions. In "A Horseman in the Sky," Bierce depicts a Federal sentinel in tormenting circumstances on the eve of an unnamed battle in western Virginia. This boy joined the Union army, the story's narrator says, over the objections of his Southern-sympathizing father, who merely enjoined him to "'do what you conceive to be your duty'" (79). Now he finds that his duty is to kill without warning and in cold blood a Confederate scout who has discovered the Union army's location; if he does not do so, his force will lose the element of surprise in the next day's fighting. Remembering his father's injunction, the sentinel steels himself, squeezes the trigger, and knowingly kills his father, who after his son's departure joined the Confederacy as a scout. In "One of the Missing" Bierce presents a Union scout who faces an equally harrowing choice in the wake of the battle of Kennesaw Mountain, a part of Sherman's Atlanta campaign. Knocked unconscious when Confederate artillery destroys the farm outbuilding in which he has posted himself, the scout awakens pinned under rubble and with his own rifle pointed at his forehead. Knowing that if he moves the rifle will go off, he sits still and waits for help, until he realizes that rats are creeping ever closer to him and will soon be gnawing upon him if he does not move. Believing that his only choice is between a quick death and a slow one, he deliberately moves to set the rifle off. He dies, but from terror, not the weapon; the story's narrator informs the reader that the rifle had discharged in the explosion that destroyed the building. He also points out that just minutes after the death Federal troops who could have rescued the scout arrive at the scene.

An even more grimly ironic fate, also involving the horrifying image of animals feeding on helpless battlefield casualties,[1] awaits Federal captain Downing Madwell in "The Coup de Grâce." Setting out alone to search for a missing friend on a bloody field immediately after an unspecified battle, Madwell finds the man mortally wounded, with scavenging hogs already chewing on him. Ravaged with pity and revulsion, Madwell musters all his nerve and drives his sword through his friend's body, only to discover, in the story's last sentence, that his arch-enemy, a Union major, along with two others, has witnessed what can be readily construed as an act of murder. Perhaps the grimmest end of all in these edge-of-battle stories, however, is the purposeful suicide of the title character in "George Thurston." This man, a Federal officer, feels a powerful urge to run away during every battle, which causes him to consider himself unworthy of his fellow officers' friendship. He masters this impulse with reckless bravery in each engagement, but he continues to isolate himself because he loathes his inability actually to rid himself of this fear, never realizing, as a result of his self-imposed isolation, that fear before every battle is the norm for most soldiers. His ultimate response to what he conceives to be his irresolvable dilemma is to eliminate his terrors by obliterating his consciousness, in the most absurd and thus most terrifying act of self-destruction he can find ready to hand. When some of the officers in his regiment mount a rope swing in a lofty tree branch, Thurston simply swings as high as he can and then lets go, silhouetting himself momentarily against the sky in his act of utterly pointless courage before he falls to his bone-shattering death.

That Bierce would focus in the majority of his war stories on men in such isolated situations—standing lonely lookout duty, performing solitary scouting missions, roaming battlefields apparently occupied only by the dead and dying, swinging through empty space—makes sense, given his propensity in all his fiction for centering his attention on the isolated, alienated individual consciousness. The seemingly empty but nevertheless potentially hostile landscape in these stories provides a perfect physical catalyst for and counterpart to the characters' mental state. We have seen, however, in "What I Saw of Shiloh" and "The Crime at Pickett's Mill," and it is further demonstrated in the behavior of George Thurston, that Bierce regards the soldier in the moment of battle as equally isolated, alienated, and mired in subjectivity, even though at that point he is surrounded by his compatriots. With this fact in mind, I will examine two of the few Bierce war stories that engage the actual moment of combat, with the aim of demonstrating that the attitudes toward history that Bierce expresses in his memoirs carry over into his fiction. In these stories, as in those memoirs, the protagonists' reliance on history and a theoretical understanding of warfare derived from history inevitably leads to death. Having read history, and believing as a result that they can behave objectively and therefore rationally and honorably on the battlefield, these protagonists are destroyed by the discovery that their responses are subjective and that they cannot surmount that fact. Cathy Davidson notes that struggles with the limitations of subjectivity are endemic to Bierce's characters; she points out that "Bierce structures nearly all of his stories around breakdowns in perception and communication" (2). Davidson also asserts that such breakdowns are especially acute in the war stories, in which the characters "are victimized not so much by some external threat as by their own inability to comprehend or cope with a seeming threat discerned in external circumstances" (11).

These assessments are entirely accurate; I take them as a starting point to suggest that the reason for the characters' inability to comprehend or cope stems from their failure to recognize that breakdowns in communication and perception are the norm on the battlefield rather than the exception and must be treated as such if one is going to survive. Nurtured on books that lead them to believe that battle can be assimilated rationally, rather than on those that more truthfully just document its irrationality, as we have seen Bierce doing in his memoirs, these protagonists attempt to override the onset of isolation in subjectivity through a recourse to their conceptions of history, which fail them utterly.

Perhaps the clearest example of such a failure is the story "One Officer, One Man," which offers a fuller look into the mind of a character beset by the doubts that are briefly said to plague George Thurston. Bierce opens with an overview of a scene that by now should strike us as a classically accurate bit of Civil War realism, an army drawn up in line of battle with the individual soldier able to see only part of his own force and nothing of the enemy. The protagonist, Captain Anderton Graffenreid, stands before his company, which is part of a series of regiments drawn up in an open field. Graffenreid can see units of his own army for perhaps two miles on either side, but the narrator notes that the battle line stretches many miles farther in both directions, disappearing into woods as it does so. To Graffenreid's front, the narrator continues, there is "not a human being visible anywhere" (207).

It is not just on this morning, however, that the enemy is invisible to Graffenreid, for the narrator says that even though this unidentified engagement takes place in 1863, "Captain Graffenreid had never in his life seen an armed enemy" (207); this is his first battle. With an ironic swipe at the army's characteristic lack of rationality, the narrator explains that Graffenreid "had had the rare advantage of a military education, and [so] when his comrades had marched to the front he had been detached for administrative service at the capital of his State, where it was thought he could be most useful," a turn of events that Graffenreid "[l]ike a bad soldier . . . protested, and like a good one obeyed" (207). If Graffenreid's theoretical grasp of warfare was thus a stumbling block in his quest to get into battle, it proves an even greater drawback when the captain finally does reach the field, for one of the untested academic concepts he brings with him is an initially praiseworthy but ultimately self-destructive vision of the relationship between soldiery and chivalry. Because his bureaucratic duties led him into a close relationship with the governor of his state, the narrator explains, Graffenreid was soon offered promotion to field rank. He refused such preferment, however, holding "a chivalrous feeling that war's rewards belonged of right to those who bore the storm and stress of battle" (207). As a result, he languished in the state capital for two years, despite his innumerable requests that he be transferred to the field at his proper rank of captain; only shortly before the story's beginning was his wish finally granted.

Although laudable in itself, Graffenreid's theoretical sense of chivalry is dangerous in practice, for it cuts him off from those around him who might acquaint him with the truth about what to expect now that he has at last reached the front. Part of Graffenreid's image of chivalry is that the good soldier never explains himself, never unburdens himself to his comrades—in particular, never offers an account of his two-year struggle to get to the battlefield. The result is that the captain, "untried by fire," now stands "in the van of a company of hardy veterans, to whom he had been only a name, and that name a by-word. By none—not even by those of his brother officers in whose favor he had waived his rights—was his devotion to duty understood. They were too busy to be just; he was looked upon as one who had shirked his duty, until forced unwillingly into the field" (208).

The price of the isolation Graffenreid has created by his reticence comes into sharper focus as Bierce develops the scene of impending battle. Having established the first of Graffenreid's theory-derived misconceptions about proper soldierly behavior in general, Bierce next reveals the gulf between Graffenreid and the rest of the army that opens as a result of Graffenreid's equal misconceptions about what a soldier feels and does in the particular circumstances of combat. The seasoned troops wait with a grimly businesslike demeanor for the onset of the battle, seeing not merely what is literally present but rather what they, as veterans, know this sight portends; the narrator says simply that although the field is empty and quiet, "every man in those miles of men knew that he and death were face to face" (207). The raw Graffenreid, however, sees and feels things much differently.

Unfamiliar with the carnage that this sight presages, he can imagine "nothing more peaceful than the appearance of that pleasant landscape with its long stretches of brown fields" (207). This failure to see beyond the field's literal appearance also has its counterpart in Graffenreid's feelings regarding what is about to take place. Not yet understanding the irrelevance of principles and ideals when one faces the arbitrariness and irrationality of death by projectile, the captain is in the highest possible spirits. While to the veterans their situation threatens death, the narrator explains that to Graffenreid "this was opportunity. . . . Victory or defeat, as God might will; in one or the other he should prove himself a soldier and a hero; he should vindicate his right to the respect of his men and the companionship of his brother officers . . ." (208).

With the first shot of the battle, however, Graffenreid loses the exultation that anticipating his own heroism has provided. A plume of smoke appears over the treetops in the army's front, followed by a "deep, jarring explosion" and a "hideous rushing sound . . . rising from whisper to roar with too quick a gradation for attention to note the successive stages of its horrible progression" (209). Faced with this threat coming at him too rapidly for rational reflection, Graffenreid dodges sharply, only to realize, an instant later, that the shell has landed far to his left. It is at this point that Graffenreid's self-created isolation begins to take its toll. Were Graffenreid not cut off from those around him, he might be able, through talking to veterans, to dismiss his overreaction as an understandable product of inexperience—or even to regard it as an involuntary response of surprise to which a veteran no less than a novice is prone, for the narrator is careful to point out a fact that Graffenreid is too startled to notice. When the shell's whine begins, the narrator says, "[a] visible tremor ran along the lines of men; all were startled into motion" (209). Graffenreid, however, focused only on himself, feels that his revelation of fear is shameful. That this high emotion drives him even further into subjective isolation is clear from the phrasing in which Bierce has the narrator detail Graffenreid's succeeding thoughts. The narrator says that Graffenreid "heard, or *fancied* he heard [emphasis added] a low, mocking laugh and turning in the direction whence it came saw the eyes of his first lieutenant fixed upon him with an unmistakable look of amusement. He looked along the line of faces in the front ranks. The men were laughing. At him?" (209).

Significantly, the narrator does not answer this question, although Graffenreid himself responds in the affirmative. Given what we have learned about his name's having become a byword for shirking, the likeliest answer is that the men *are* laughing at Graffenreid but are equally amused at their own discomfiture. Involuntary dodging is not shameful but normal, a subject for laughter as much of relief as of derision. Graffenreid, however, has no way of discovering this fact, for his own historically implanted sense that he ought to behave as a hero has cut him off not only from any ability to appraise his own behavior realistically but also from any potential for developing that ability through interaction with others.

The increasing irony of Graffenreid's condition becomes apparent as the captain considers his response to the shell. Graffenreid had not known, the narrator says, "that the flight of a projectile was a phenomenon of so appalling character," and as a result, "[h]is conception of war had already undergone a profound change" (209). Like any other soldier under fire for the first time, Graffenreid has discovered the true, terrifying character of war; it is time to discard his illusions and face the facts, that his feelings of fear and disorientation are entirely natural to his situation. But his isolation continues to serve him badly. Unable to communicate with those around him, Graffenreid has no way of learning that his response is normal, that it is not he himself but his expectations of himself that are at fault. Instead, he sees his responses as weakness outside the norm of soldierly behavior.

At first, Graffenreid hesitates to put a name to his new feeling about war; he is only aware that it "was manifesting itself in visible perturbation. His blood was boiling in his veins; he had a choking sensation and felt that if he had a command to give it would be inaudible, or at least unintelligible" (209–10). He then forces himself to identify this feeling, but again, as in the passage detailing his first response to what he believes to be his men's perception of him, the phrasing is such that it emphasizes the subjective nature of his analysis. Graffenreid "found a difficulty in standing still," the narrator says, "and *fancied* that his men observed it [emphasis added]. Was it fear? He feared it was" (210). Unfortunately for himself, Graffenreid has learned only that he himself feels fear, not that fear is commonplace on the battlefield—that fear is not to be feared but accepted, even laughed at. Rather than discarding his historically based illusions about soldierly behavior, an act from which he is prevented by one of those very illusions—that the good soldier does not communicate his feelings to others—he mistakenly retains them, measures himself by them, and decides that he falls short.

Graffenreid shortly finds even stronger reasons to condemn himself in his response to his first sight of a dead man. Soon after the cannon shot that has caused him such consternation, the still-invisible enemy opens with musketry from the woods. The seasoned troops respond to their officers' immediate orders to lie down with an alacrity that should make the captain reconsider his belief that his earlier flinching before the shell constituted cowardice. He fails to make such a reconsideration, however, because the one man shot in this firing was standing next to him in the line of battle; when Graffenreid drops to the ground he finds himself eye to sightless eye with a corpse, a situation that occupies his full attention. Hugging the earth, Graffenreid sees that beneath the dead man's breast "flowed a little rill of blood [which] . . . had a faint sweetish order that sickened him. The face was crushed into the earth and flattened. It looked yellow already, and was repulsive" (211).

Once more, the moment is right for Graffenreid to let go of his illusions about battle and soldierly behavior, for their falsity literally stares him in the face. Nothing about the corpse, the narrator says, "suggested the glory of a soldier's death nor mitigated the loathsomeness of the incident" (211). Yet again, however, Graffenreid clings to his illusions, finding himself wanting instead; he persists in his belief that battle ought to be glorious and that its not being so is somehow a matter of his response to it rather than anything to do with its essential nature. As the captain lies on his stomach and determinedly avoids looking again at the corpse, the narrator continues, "[t]he fire of battle was not now burning very brightly in this warrior's soul. From inaction had come introspection. He sought rather to analyze his feelings than distinguish himself by courage and devotion. The result was profoundly disappointing. He covered his face with his hands and groaned aloud" (211).

Thus far, Graffenreid's military education, his understanding of military history, has proven a distinct disadvantage. Earlier, we saw that De Forest presents himself and his fictional counterpart Colburne as likewise having had a military education, and it is at this moment in their own experiences, when they are first confronted with the imminent prospect of sudden death—or actually slightly before it, before they are overwhelmed by subjective responses as Graffenreid is—that their education comes to their rescue. Their sense of history, in the form of Army Regulations, renews their awareness of their obligations to the men in their charge, thus blocking them off from morbid introspection by reminding them of their connections to others. The sense in which history comes to Graffenreid's rescue, however, is bitterly ironic, in keeping with Bierce's own attitudes toward history and the way the author has therefore depicted Graffenreid as allowing history to play him false thus far.

Graffenreid's theoretical military education evidently focused exclusively on the individual's behavior rather than on the principles of unit cohesion and interdependent responsibilities, or perhaps his image of his own ideal demeanor is all the captain remembers at this moment of stress. In either case, Graffenreid is already beyond the point at which he might establish productive contact with his men through a vision of combat larger than his own place in it, a fact Bierce makes clear in his final portrait of the captain. The firing to the front of Graffenreid's battalion ceases, the narrator explains, while the sounds of battle rise to "a roar, . . . a thunder" (211) off to the right. The field officers in command of Graffenreid's position can see nothing of what is happening on the right, of course, but they surmise that their army must be advancing there and so order Graffenreid's battalion to stand again, re-form, and prepare to push forward in support of the right wing's success. It is at this point that the reader gets a final sight of Graffenreid, from an angle that emphasizes his now-complete self-absorption and concomitantly increasing mental deterioration, for his thoughts at this moment of actual engagement for which he has waited so long focus solely on his subjective analysis of his circumstances and himself. The narrator says, "Captain Graffenreid stood at the head of his company, the dead man at his feet. He heard the battle on the right—rattle and crash of musketry, ceaseless thunder of cannon, desultory cheers of invisible combatants. He marked ascending clouds of smoke from distant forests. He noted the sinister silence of the forest in front" (212).

On the one hand, Graffenreid continues to perceive certain things in a way that accords with his illusions, such as the far-off firing and cheering, the rising smoke; at a distance, battle seems still to conform to his expectations. On the other hand, however, he confronts immediately before him the actuality of combat, its hideous meaninglessness, in the dead man and the menacingly inexpressive quality of the forest. Rejecting one or the other of these visions, or else synthesizing them, proves impossible for Graffenreid. Refusing to let go of his illusions, he simply breaks down. The narrator explains that "[t]hese contrasting extremes affected the whole range of [Graffenreid's] sensibilities. The strain upon his nervous organization was insupportable. He grew hot and cold by turns. He panted like a dog, and then forgot to breathe until reminded by vertigo" (212).

Graffenreid here draws on history for help, but with tragic results rather than the steadying influence that he expects and that is found in De Forest's depictions of his own and Colburne's turnings to the past. Utterly disoriented, feeling himself a coward and seeking expiation, the captain suddenly perceives his salvation in what is, in his mind, a long-standing, noble military tradition. As De Forest and his characters so frequently do, Graffenreid conjures up images of the martial spirit of ancient Rome. In phrasing that once again emphasizes the subjectivity of Graffenreid's vision, the narrator says that, in the throes of his breakdown, "[s]uddenly [Graffenreid] grew calm. Glancing downward, his eyes had fallen upon his naked sword, as he held it, point to earth. Fore-shortened to his view, it resembled somewhat, he thought, the short heavy blade of the ancient Roman. The fancy was full of suggestion, malign, fateful, heroic!" (212). The narrator continues,

> The sergeant in the rear rank, immediately behind Captain Graffenreid, now observed a strange sight. His attention drawn by an uncommon movement made by the captain—a sudden reaching forward of the hands and their energetic withdrawal, throwing the elbows out, as in pulling an oar—he saw spring from between the officer's shoulders a bright point of metal which prolonged itself outward, nearly a half-arm's length—a blade! . . . That moment Captain Graffenreid pitched heavily forward upon the dead man and died. (212–13)

That Graffenreid's final recourse to history here is not heroic but meaningless is driven home by the coda Bierce provides to this gesture. Although

Graffenreid dies believing he has at last demonstrated his worthiness to be a soldier through his unyielding adherence to his illusion of martial Roman atonement, his death makes no impression. The story ends, like "Jupiter Doke," with an official dispatch that puts all its events into their proper perspective. A week after the engagement in which Graffenreid made his supposedly noble gesture, the general commanding that part of the battle line in which the captain served sends this missive to his superior: "'Sir: I have the honor to report, with regard to the action of the 19th inst., that owing to the enemy's withdrawal from my front to reinforce his beaten left, my command was not seriously engaged. My loss was as follows: Killed, one officer, one man'" (213). Graffenreid's suicide is doubly pointless in light of this dispatch. The captain killed himself to prove his worthiness to participate in an assault that never occurred, and his name does not even survive. He will have no monument in his beloved history, a fitting fate, in Bierce's view, for those who put their trust in history in the first place.[2]

My comments on "One Officer, One Man" have emphasized the fact that Graffenreid destroys himself through his failure to communicate with his fellow soldiers, through his inability to attain the sense of belonging to the group by which, in S. L. A. Marshall's words, "every man is in aid in helping [the individual] choke down the fear which might otherwise have stopped him" (47). Given the terms in which Bierce casts this particular story, such an assessment is accurate. In the larger context of all Bierce's war stories, however, the individual soldier's sharing a consciousness with the others of his unit offers no more hope of survival than does isolation. The essential mistake for Graffenreid is an attempt to use history to combat his individual subjectivity. In Bierce's view, the group's consciousness is equally subjective and thus equally likely to fall prey to a misguided recourse to history.

In the second chapter of this study, I noted Marshall's belief that positive bonds among the members of a force are a necessary condition for that force to function effectively; Marshall's formulation is that "the tactical unity of men working together in combat will be in the ratio of their knowledge and sympathetic understanding of each other" (150). Bierce's response to this notion is clear enough in his depiction of group consciousness at work in the story "One Kind of Officer." The narrator of this story points out that "[a]n army has a personality. Beneath the individual thoughts and emotions of its component parts it thinks and feels as a unit. And in this large, inclusive sense of things lies a wiser wisdom than the mere sum of all it knows" (195).

Thus far, Bierce's findings appear to be in accord with Marshall's. Bierce's use of the term "wiser wisdom," however, has a sarcastic edge, for in his eyes this "wisdom" is no guarantee of tactical efficiency. Rather, it is simply an animal-like instinct that produces a sense of uneasiness because the army as a whole in combat is, like the individual, painfully aware of its inability to understand its own circumstances, a result of both immediate limitations of vision and lack of military education. For Bierce, in other words, an army's group knowledge is merely its collective recognition that, although it can see little and understands almost nothing of the strategic and tactical implications of what it does see, there is nonetheless much threat in its circumstances.

This viewpoint is clear in what follows the above-mentioned passage from "One Kind of Officer." On the day this story takes place, the narrator continues, "this great brute force"—that is, the army's aggregate personality—

> groping at the bottom of a white ocean of fog among trees that seemed as sea weeds, had a dumb consciousness that all was not well; that a day's manoeuvring had resulted in a faulty disposition of its parts, a blind diffusion of its strength. The men felt insecure and talked among themselves of such tactical errors as with their meager military vocabulary they were able to name. Field and line officers gathered in groups and spoke no more learnedly of what they apprehended with no greater clearness. Commanders of brigades and divisions looked anxiously to their connections on the right and on the left, sent staff officers on errands of inquiry and pushed skirmish lines silently and cautiously forward into the dubious region between the known and the unknown. (195–96)

Plainly, these men know and understand one another, but this sympathy is merely a shared awareness of a threatening subjectivity, not the steadying force for objectivity it might be in "One Officer, One Man."

Bierce does not explore the ramifications of this view of an army's collective personality in "One Kind of Officer"; he merely mentions them in passing. However, a thorough examination of the dangerous effects of group responses is to be found in the story "A Son of the Gods." In this account, based on Bierce's own experience,[3] an officer finds himself in much the same situation as Captain Graffenreid in "One Officer, One Man": being regarded as deficient at the outset of a battle by the men with whom he serves. Instead of falling into Graffenreid's reaction and further isolating himself, however, this officer makes himself part of the group through a courageous action perhaps motivated not by illusions derived from history but by his regard both for the welfare of his fellows and for their opinion of him; the latter is another important component of the group consciousness, according to Marshall.[4] But this response proves as tragically futile as Graffenreid's, for even if the officer's response is not conditioned by history, his very acceptance by the group draws that group unwittingly into a reaction that *is* conditioned by history, to an even more damaging extent than Graffenreid's is.

The comparison between "One Officer, One Man" and "A Son of the Gods" is sharpened from the outset by the fact that the latter story, like the former, begins with the classically realistic Civil War–story picture of part of an army—again a Union army—drawn up in line of battle to face it knows not what. Only one difference obtains: this time the army is in the woods rather than the open, and it is the open space that poses the invisible threat. The first-person narrator, a Union officer on the staff of the corps commander in charge of this force, establishes the scene in the story's first paragraph:

> A breezy day and a sunny landscape. An open country to right and left and forward; behind, a wood. In the edge of this wood, facing the open but not venturing into it, long lines of troops, halted.... Detached groups of horsemen are well in front—not altogether exposed—many of them intently regarding the crest of a hill a mile away in the direction of the interrupted advance. For this powerful army, moving through a forest, has met with a formidable obstacle—the open country. The crest of that gentle hill a mile away has a wall extending to left and right a great distance. Behind the wall is a hedge; behind the hedge are seen the tops of

trees in rather straggling order. Among the trees—what? It is necessary to know. (108)

At this point, with the army's need for knowledge established, the character for whom the story is titled, one of the narrator's fellow Federal officers, makes his appearance. Although Bierce's use of a first-person narrator here precludes the reader's access to this character's thoughts, the officer appears from his attire to harbor the same kind of historically derived illusions about military glory as Graffenreid does, for he has appointed himself in a fashion as close to that of a knight-errant as he can attain in the nineteenth century. As the general commanding the corps and his staff discuss ways to address their need to know what lies beyond the distant trees, the narrator reports, this young officer rides up, mounted on a "snow-white horse" gaily caparisoned with a scarlet saddle blanket, and himself "in full uniform, as if on parade. He is all agleam with bullion—a blue-and-gold edition of the Poetry of War" (110).

Initially, this officer evokes the same reaction from others as Graffenreid, for he appears to understand no more of the reality of war than that well-educated neophyte. The narrator remarks, "What a fool! No one who has ever been in action but remembers how naturally every rifle turns toward the man on a white horse; no one but has observed how a bit of red enrages the bull of battle. That such colors are fashionable in military life must be accepted as the most astonishing of all the phenomena of human vanity" (110). That the veterans in the halted army's ranks share this assessment is clear, for as the overdressed youth canters toward the general's party, the narrator reports, "A wave of derisive laughter runs abreast of him all along the line" (110).

Despite these snide responses, however, an afterthought from the narrator reveals that even such hardened veterans are not immune to the lure of the battlefield romanticism that this young cavalier appears to them to represent. The final comment the narrator offers regarding his own and the troops' view of this figure is "But how handsome he is!—with what careless grace he sits his horse" (110). If this comment indicates an inclination on the army's part to retract its rejection, the officer's subsequent action transforms this inclination into an overwhelming desire. As the officer rides toward the general, the latter dispatches a line of skirmishers to push out of the woods and into the open to discover what, if anything, lies among the looming trees beyond the hill. Again using his first-person narrator's limited perspective to screen the reader from access to the young officer's thoughts, for reasons that will shortly become apparent, Bierce depicts that officer's gesture that stops those skirmishers. The young man, the narrator says,

> reins up within a respectful distance of the corps commander and salutes. . . . A brief colloquy between them is going on; the young man seems to be preferring some request which the elder one is indisposed to grant. Let us ride a little nearer. Ah! too late—it is ended. The young officer salutes again, wheels his horse, and rides straight toward the crest of the hill!
>
> . . . The commander speaks to his bugler, who claps his instrument to his lips. Tra-la-la! Tra-la-la! The skirmishers halt in their tracks.
>
> Meantime the young horseman has advanced a hundred yards. He is riding at a walk, straight up the long slope, with never a turn of the head. (110–11)

The meaning of these movements quickly dawns on the troops: the young officer is riding ahead alone to investigate the hill, wall, and trees. This action means certain death if Confederates are lying in ambush, for they cannot allow the scout to return and report on their position. Such a death will be a generous self-sacrifice, however, for by killing the young officer the Confederates will reveal their position as surely as if they were to allow him to return, and he will thereby save the lives not just of the skirmishing party but of the entire army. Suddenly the Union force not only accepts this young man as a part of its collective consciousness but makes him the focus of that consciousness, and the trappings of his dress that looked foolish a moment before now look like the proper attire for a son of the gods of battle. In terms that emphasize that he is describing the army's collective response, the narrator exclaims,

> How glorious! Gods! what we would not give to be in his place—with his soul! He does not draw a sabre; his right hand hangs easily at his

side. The breeze catches the plume in his hat and flutters it smartly. The sunshine rests upon his shoulder-straps, lovingly, like a visible benediction. Straight on he rides. Ten thousand pairs of eyes are fixed upon him with an intensity that he can hardly fail to feel; ten thousand hearts keep quick time to the inaudible hoof-beats of his snowy steed. He is not alone—he draws all souls after him. But we remember that we laughed! On and on, straight for the hedge-lined wall, he rides. Not a look backward. O, if he would but turn—if he could but see the love, the adoration, the atonement! (111)

Unlike Graffenreid, then, this young officer has become one with the rest of the army; in so doing he appears to have transcended isolation enforced by historically planted illusions about battle. But in fact it is possible that he has not so much transcended these illusions as, by the sheer theatricality of his gesture, instead momentarily drawn every man in the onlooking corps into sharing them. That the troops' feelings about this action contradict their usual reaction to battle is clear from the narrator's description of their continued response as the young officer nears the danger zone of hill and wall. "All these hardened and impenitent man-killers," the narrator says, "to whom death in its awfulest forms is a fact familiar to their everyday observation; who sleep on hills trembling with the thunder of great guns, dine in the midst of streaming missiles, and play cards among the dead faces of their dearest friends—all are watching with suspended breath and beating hearts the outcome of an act involving the life of one man. Such is the magnetism of courage and devotion" (111–12).

This magnetism is such, in fact, that the army of impenitent man-killers even attaches religious significance to the officer's action, despite its surroundings and circumstances. When the possibility of ambush lies ahead, the narrator continues,

> [t]he natural and customary thing to do is to send forward a line of skirmishers. But in this case they will answer in the affirmative with all their lives; the enemy, crouching double ranks behind the stone wall and in cover of the hedge, will wait until it is possible to count the assailant's teeth. At the first volley a half of the questioning line will fall, the other half before it can accomplish the predestined retreat.

> What a price to pay for gratified curiosity! At what a dear rate an army must sometimes purchase knowledge! "Let me pay all," says this gallant man—this military Christ! (112–13)

It is at this point, with all the soldiers utterly responsive to this instance of individual heroism despite their usual indifference to single deaths, that the dangers of the group consciousness, a result of its being as subjective and irrational as the individual consciousness, become apparent. Bierce has kept the officer's motives for this sacrifice obscure in order to emphasize that the army's response to it, based on insufficient knowledge of its reasons, is entirely subjective. The officer's own view of his action may be completely rational—it is possible, as M. E. Grenander suggests, that this young man has shed any illusions of heroism and is simply taking a calculated risk to save lives (120). It is equally possible that, given the evidence of his dress, the officer is in fact attempting to live out, however briefly, an unrealistic notion of personal heroism. In either case, the point is that the other soldiers do not know the reason; as the rest of the story reveals, they simply respond, despite their deep understanding of battle's realities, to their own newly awakened (or perhaps reawakened) romantic concept of individual heroism, which leads to pointless wholesale slaughter and makes the officer's action, whatever its motivations, utterly futile. For a brief, deadly moment, the army as a whole is as heedless of the consequences of war as the deaf-mute child at the beginning of "Chickamauga."

Inevitably, the narrator says, the courageous young officer dies, albeit in an unusually spectacular manner that continues to compel the entire army's attention. This passage is worth quoting at length to demonstrate the intensity of the soldiers' feelings that pave the way for their irrational response to this death. The officer reaches the wall and sees enough to confirm the troops' collective fear of ambush:

> One moment only and he wheels right about and is speeding like the wind straight down the slope—toward his friends, toward his death! Instantly the wall is topped with a fierce roll of smoke for a distance of hundreds of yards to right and left. This is as instantly dissipated by the wind, and before the rattle of the rifles reaches us he is down. No, he recovers his seat; he has but pulled his horse upon its haunches.

They are up and away! A tremendous cheer bursts from our ranks, relieving the insupportable tension of our feelings. And the horse and its rider? Yes, they are up and away. Away, indeed—they are making directly to our left, parallel to the now steadily blazing and smoking wall. The rattle of the musketry is continuous, and every bullet's target is that courageous heart.

Suddenly a great bank of white smoke pushes upward from behind the wall. Another and another—a dozen roll up before the thunder of the explosions and the humming of the missiles reach our ears and the missiles themselves come bounding through clouds of dust into our covert. . . .

The dust drifts away. Incredible!—that enchanted horse and rider have passed a ravine and are climbing another slope to unveil another conspiracy of silence, to thwart the will of another armed host. Another moment and that crest too is in eruption. The horse rears and strikes the air with its forefeet. They are down at last. But look again—the man has detached himself from the dead animal. He stands erect, motionless, holding his sabre in his right hand straight above his head. His face is toward us. Now he lowers his hand to a level with his face and moves it outward, the blade of the sabre describing a downward curve. It is a sign to us, to the world, to posterity. It is a hero's salute to death and history. (114–15)

If the narrator's belief that the dying officer is saluting history is correct, the evidence suggests that his actions are not rational but the product of historically derived illusions regarding heroism and the gaining of personal glory. What is certain is that this final gesture drives the men into a reaction that is utterly irrational, the product of their own historically instilled response to the idea of individual heroism. The officer's presumable goal was to save lives, but his last action guarantees that this goal will not be attained; the men's response is so intense that they are driven to seek immediate revenge for his death at the cost of their own lives. With the dying officer's salute, the narrator says,

> the spell is broken; our men attempt to cheer; they are choking with emotion; they utter hoarse, discordant cries; they clutch their

weapons and press tumultuously forward into the open. The skirmishers, without orders, against orders, are going forward at a keen run, like hounds unleashed. Our cannon speak and the enemy's now open in full chorus; to right and left as far as we can see, the distant crest, now seeming so near, erects its towers of cloud and the great shot pitch roaring down among our moving masses. Flag after flag of ours emerges from the wood, line after line sweeps forth, catching the sunlight on its burnished arms. (115)

The general, witnessing this pointless assault against a well-shielded enemy, immediately orders his buglers to sound the recall. However, by the time the sound penetrates the unreasoning battle-frenzy the young officer's actions have whipped the troops into, many men have been killed and wounded—certainly more than would have fallen had the skirmishers revealed the ambush in a less romantic manner, and perhaps more even than if the army had simply blundered ahead without putting forward any feelers. To an even greater extent here than in "One Officer, One Man," a recourse in battle to historically based illusions leads to destruction, with the added points that the group is no less susceptible than the isolated individual to such illusions and that, as Cathy Davidson says regarding Bierce's stories in general, "if experience is the best teacher, . . . it is still not a very good one" (66). But Bierce does not stop with these insights in "A Son of the Gods"; a still grimmer corollary comes in the story's closing paragraph. The narrator's remarks here suggest that, regardless of their deadliness, illusions may be the only things a man can cling to in battle, for his final comment on the whole action is a lament that the young officer, seeing his fellows rush into a suicidal attack, dies as a result with a sense of disillusionment. "Ah," the narrator concludes, "those many, many needless dead! That great soul whose beautiful body is lying over yonder, so conspicuous against the sere hillside—could it not have been spared the bitter consciousness of a vain devotion? Would one exception have marred too much the pitiless perfection of the divine, eternal plan?" (116).[5]

Given this valediction, we might logically conclude that, taken together, "One Officer, One Man" and "A Son of the Gods" reveal Bierce's belief that the individual in battle has no escape from death. Whether he remains isolated or seeks the comfort of a group consciousness, whether he faces his first battle or has passed through dozens, he will inevitably fall victim to some form of illusion. Fate, in the guise of the burden of some conception of history, will get him at last. Such a conclusion gains further plausibility when we consider that Bierce provides yet another example of the myriad ways the illusions of history may operate to destroy the individual in the story "Killed at Resaca." This tale describes the military life and death of Union Lieutenant Herman Brayle, an excellent soldier, by the narrator's account, except that he is "vain of his courage" (134), a trait manifested in his habit of recklessly making himself the target of enemy fire at every opportunity, even when doing so is not necessary, rather than taking the more soldierly approach of seeking any available cover to maximize his chances of living to fight another day. Inevitably, Brayle dies—as the narrator says, "[H]e who ignores the law of probabilities challenges an adversary that is seldom beaten" (136)—and does so in a manner very similar to that of the young officer in "A Son of the Gods": he gallops dramatically across open ground in defiance of the enemy's guns, a gesture that leads one hundred of his fellow Federals to sacrifice their own lives in a pointless effort to avenge him. As in "A Son of the Gods," Bierce's argument here is that even when veterans have wisely discarded any desire to prove their own heroism by some conventional but meaningless gesture, they may well be drawn in by a response to someone else's still-maintained illusion that such a gesture is the only proof of courage.

In "Killed at Resaca," however, there is yet another layer of irony beyond that displayed in "A Son of the Gods." No less than the soldiers in both stories who respond to someone else's illusion, Brayle himself, the narrator indicates, had discarded his own illusions; he dies as a result of someone else's. After the battle, the narrator receives Brayle's pocketbook from the army's commander as a memento of the fallen officer. In it he finds a letter to Brayle from a young woman in San Francisco, Brayle's former home. He quotes what is, to him, the letter's most significant paragraph: "'Mr. Winters, whom I shall always hate for it, has been telling that at some battle in Virginia, where he got his hurt, you were seen crouching behind a tree. I think he wants to injure you in my regard, which he knows the story would do if I believed it. I could bear to hear of my soldier lover's death, but not of his cowardice'" (140). Early on in his military career, Brayle himself had evidently learned to let go of any notion that reckless behavior is the same thing as courage. Yet this illusion, in the form of a rival's jealousy and a woman's misconceptions about the true nature of battle, still stretches out its hand—from a distance of three thousand miles—and destroys him.

The belief readily fostered by these three tales, and indeed by all of Bierce's war stories, is that Bierce sees the soldier's life as utterly hopeless. As Eric Solomon states the case, Bierce limns "the blackest side of war," in which "[m]an in all his insignificance learns the futility of 'normal' actions and aspirations in the face of the all-encompassing universe" of combat—in which "[t]he outcome of his most valiant efforts is usually failure" (*Banners* 212). This assessment accords well with the viewpoint of the many critics who limit their perspective on this writer to the frequently employed tag "bitter Bierce." They assert that, as depicted in such stories as these, the physical and psychological horrors of Bierce's Civil War service, being the dominant formative experiences of his life, are responsible for the unrelieved grimness of his stories in general. Solomon argues that Bierce's youth at the time of his enlistment explains the war's destructive effect upon his outlook; at eighteen, Solomon says, Bierce was "young enough for the ironies of war to become an integral part of his education" ("Bitterness" 183). Daniel Aaron's assessment is similar, but it focuses more specifically on Bierce's writings and is more colorfully expressed: "Ambrose Bierce not only choked on the blood of the Civil War, he nearly drowned in it. For the remainder of his life it bubbled in his imagination and stained his prose" ("Civil War" 171). Larzer Ziff goes even further in this vein, contending that not only did Bierce not learn to write about war from books, he learned to write books from war. Ziff quotes Bierce's assertion that "the good writer (supposing him to be born to the trade) is not made by reading, but by observing and experiencing." This belief, Ziff says, "meant that . . . Bierce . . . had little to learn from other writers, and it also meant that his wartime experiences could be held in suspension and made to stand for all the books and all the other experiences life could afford. . . . [W]ar, which abounded in violent reversals, became the pattern of life, and everything that occurred outside his window could be accounted for, as were events in war, as the chance happenings of a universe in which moral causation bore no relation to events" (168). So widespread is this view that critics even quote other critics with regard to it, as is the case in John R. Brazil's 1980 reference to Paul Fatout's 1951 biography of Bierce, *The Devil's Lexicographer*. Brazil notes that "Bierce emerged from the war with what Paul Fatout has termed a 'defective mental vision'—a vision that constricted his perception to the vicious in life" (226).

That many critics would adopt this reading of Bierce's opinion of war—and, concomitantly, of the soldier's chances in war—is understandable, particularly when it is not only evident in the stories under discussion but also carries the implicit sanction of Bierce's own brother Albert, who claimed that the head wound Bierce sustained at the battle of Kennesaw Mountain in 1864 completely changed his hitherto pleasant character, turning him toward the misanthropy for which he became famous in his later years. Interviewed by George Sterling for an article entitled "The Shadow Maker," which appeared in the October 1925 issue of the *American Mercury,* Albert said of this wound that Ambrose "was never the same after that. Some of the iron of that shell seemed to stick in his brain, and he became bitter and suspicious, especially of his close friends" (qtd. in Grattan 17).

This interpretation, however, fails to take into account a central fact of Bierce's war experience: the bitterness of many of his stories and memoirs notwithstanding, Bierce in fact throve on army life and warfare. Solomon, despite his assertion of the blackening effect of the war upon Bierce's character, acknowledges that if the young man "was revolted, intellectually, by the harsh brutalities of a repellent, paradoxical world," he nonetheless "enjoyed the test of combat, the companionship and the excitement" ("Bitterness" 190). Similarly, Lawrence Berkove says that Bierce detested romantic, sentimental expressions of patriotism and heroism and glorifications of combat, but at bottom "he was ambivalent about war. His reason opposed it; his emotions were exhilarated by it" (Introduction ix). And in spite of the quotation by Brazil, which is taken out of context, Fatout is likewise emphatic on this point. "A belief reiterated to weariness by miscellaneous analysts," Fatout says,

> is that [Bierce] was embittered by early hardships, but that theory collapses in the face of [his] cheerful acceptance of greater hardships in the army than he ever met [in his boyhood] on the farm. Far from making him bitter, [these army hardships] made him aggressive, even

gay; he was proud of youthful energy that endured long marches and lethal battles—proud, too, of his clean record, for not one demerit was ever chalked up against him. The boy and youth incited to rebellion by parental authority was as a soldier, subordinated to a stern taskmaster [General Hazen], more nearly at peace with himself and with his world than he had ever been under his parents' roof. . . . Undoubtedly he was deeply sensitive to the madness of carnage and destruction, yet the dominant note in his war recollections is of a full-bodied joy of living. (45–46)

To refer to the tone of the stories and memoirs considered thus far as expressive of a "joy of living" is perhaps excessive, yet Fatout's statement as a whole raises several questions highly relevant to those stories and memoirs. If Bierce does in fact see the individual soldier as inevitably doomed by historical illusions, how did he himself escape death to document this fact? How, for that matter, did any soldier escape? And why, if Bierce's view is so bleak, do we discern, if not joy, certainly an ambivalence about war in much of Bierce's writing? In the late story "A Resumed Identity," to consider just one example, the protagonist, like Bierce himself a former member of General Hazen's staff, revisits the battlefield of Stone River after nearly fifty years; so strongly does he find himself drawn back to that battle, as part of the only worthwhile period of his life, in his view, that he gives way to hallucinations and believes that he is once again participating in this conflict.

The answers to these questions lie in the fact that the visions underlying what happens to the characters who do not survive the war in these stories are not Bierce's own; they belong to those characters. These figures perish not because of war itself, ultimately, but because they do not let go of their own illusions—or someone else's—about it. Their problem is that they stubbornly refuse to give up the attempt to impose meaning on a meaningless experience; as Larzer Ziff notes, for Bierce "war . . . was impersonal, and the recurrent theme of his art was the way personality went smash in its failure to comprehend this" (172). Bierce himself, on the other hand, comprehended this fact and, as several perceptive critics have noted, abandoned early on the attempt to impose any sort of conventional, historical meaning on his experiences. His years as a soldier taught him many things, Berkove points out, "including the lesson that war is both foolish and terrible, that its glamour is an illusion, and that the fine talk justifying it on the grounds of patriotism and idealism is all lies" (Introduction ix). The next lesson he drew was that the soldier who operates in combat with the first lesson in mind, who lets go of all patriotism, idealism, and other preconceptions and simply acts because he has to, in a manner that a later generation would call existential, earns two prizes: a chance—albeit not a very good one—at survival, and the possibility of living, at least momentarily, the most intense life a man may aspire to. As Mary E. Grenander states this case, the man in Bierce's world confronted with life's meaninglessness, which is at its most apparent in the impersonal charnel house that is the battlefield, faces "the ultimate existential anxiety. As a living, sentient organism he must act, with such awareness and such understanding as he can muster of forces that are frequently dark and mysterious. . . . But during that stark agony, as at no other time, he discovers who he is, what life is, and what it means to be. If he lives at all after that—and he may not—he will . . . never again be the same" (77).

What existential behavior on the battlefield consists of for Bierce is a focus on just one of the several means by which combat psychologists assert that men under fire control their fears and continue to function: an intense concentration on the immediately practical matters of being a soldier. This belief is apparent in one of his *Examiner* columns commenting on other writers' reporting of the Spanish-American War. Here, as in many other columns, Bierce lambastes reporters who do not know enough about war to describe it accurately, including actions that take place right before their eyes, as is the case when they romanticize soldiers' dispassionate professionalism into bravery. "I venture to submit," Bierce observes,

> that the enthusiastic young gentlemen who send us military news from the several war-centers are a trifle too repetitive in their praise of "coolness." In every engagement on sea or land they are profoundly affected by the tranquil self-possession of our officers in the "hail of shot and shell" or "storm of bullets." It would be interesting to know how these admiring scribes think that an officer in the practice of his profession under these entirely normal conditions might naturally be expected to act. Do they look for him to gnash his teeth, tear his hair, roll his

eyes and stamp like a beeherder that has mistaken his vocation? Would it be more in accordance with the laws of nature and the fitness of things for him to pass the few precious moments of actual fighting in dodging bullets and yelling unintelligible warnings to the men he has undertaken to direct and supervise? Possibly the correspondents have not learned that the first and most elementary duty of an officer in action is to keep his head on straight and his heart out of his mouth. (Qtd. in *Skepticism* 88–89)

Bierce here sounds more like the De Forest of "The First Time Under Fire," keeping his own head at the sight of a wounded man by reminding himself of his duty to prevent his men from becoming demoralized, than he does the Bierce who withdraws into the isolation of subjectivity in "What I Saw of Shiloh." Yet there is still a clear-cut difference between these men's approaches to retaining one's composure under fire. In De Forest's view the good soldier remains in control of himself by managing battle intellectually, through recourse to his reading of realistic military history and other forms of preparatory training. In Bierce's view, on the other hand, such preparation does no good, for battle has no meaning that can be managed intellectually, either in the heat of the moment or later in a history book. History is pointless, and conventional concepts of heroism or "coolness" are pointless; the good soldier controls himself not through any such notions or through concepts of the rightness of his cause, but rather simply because, as the *Examiner* passage indicates, the only alternative is to lose control. If De Forest's definition of a hero is a man who fears death and mutilation but confronts them out of reverence for his traditional duty and honor as a soldier, out of a sense of the discipline of his profession, perhaps an alternate conception offered by Robert Glen Deamer in a discussion of Stephen Crane's and Ernest Hemingway's visions comes close to expressing Bierce's definition. "The discipline of a profession," Deamer says, "is . . . a means by which certain individuals—heroes, heroines—impose a *self-created* [emphasis added], albeit limited and finite, coherence upon a world of chaos and casualty" (149).

It is worth noting in this regard that, although De Forest does not ever depict his characters as being aided by altruistic or patriotic thoughts while under fire, he does on a larger level present all the action of *Miss Ravenel's Conversion* as taking place as part of a crusade to free the slaves and concomitantly to raise white Southerners out of the degraded state into which they have sunk as a result of the immorality of holding other human beings in bondage. Bierce, on the other hand, never mentions any larger purpose to the fighting he details in his memoirs and stories. In one of his few comments on the subject, recorded in Fatout's biography (36), he asserts that he joined the army primarily as a result of a boyish thirst for adventure. Bierce also offers a trenchant comment in an *Examiner* column from the period of the Spanish-American War concerning civilian patriots who were forming what was, in his view, a ludicrous cult around the American flag. "God bless them," he observes of such people, "how they would be shocked to observe the indifference with which it [the flag] is regarded by soldiers in battle!" (qtd. in *Skepticism* 56). Facing enemy fire calmly for no particular reason is not a desirable state of affairs, but it is still better than giving way to illusions that there are reasons to do so, in the manner of these civilians, and of Captain Graffenreid, Lieutenant Brayle, and the men who follow Brayle and the young officer in "A Son of the Gods" to their deaths. The good soldier—the professional soldier—accepts the meaninglessness of his situation as a given and carries on as best he can in spite of it rather than attempting to remedy it.

This approach in Bierce's fiction and memoirs boils down to one simple maxim. When the soldier on the battlefield finds himself unable to understand his circumstances, threatened with an inability to act as a result of his being mired in subjectivity, he need only remember that his essential duty is to move toward the area where he hears the heaviest firing going on—to march toward the sound of the guns, in a locution usually attributed in its original form to Napoleon's chief of cavalry, Joachim Murat. Bierce demonstrates this principle in action most explicitly in one of his memoirs, "A Little of Chickamauga." The "Little" of the title is a reference, like "What I Saw of Shiloh," to the only partial vision any individual can claim of any battle in which he participated; with another slap at the notion of a putatively all-encompassing history, Bierce explains that his goal is not such an account but rather "only to relate some part of what I saw of it" (32).

What Bierce saw on the first day of this two-day engagement was the utter collapse of the Union army's line of battle.[6] Through a misunderstanding of orders, Bierce explains, one Union division was withdrawn from the battle line, creating a half-mile gap, just at the moment that the Confederates mounted a full-scale frontal attack. The Confederates poured through this gap unopposed, splitting the Union army in half and throwing the right half into confusion and rout. Bierce snidely remarks that General Rosecrans, the Union commander, gave way to partial vision at this juncture, riding back to Chattanooga among the remnants of his right and telegraphing to Washington that his army had been destroyed. In actuality, Bierce notes with bitter understatement, "[t]he rest of his army was standing its ground" (35).

It is at this point that Bierce's proto-existential maxim comes into focus. Bierce explains that the rest of the Union army, the left, held firm for two reasons: the steadiness with which its commander, General Thomas, continued to conduct himself, in contrast to Rosecrans; and the fact that many of the troops from the demoralized right, rather than retreating, simply marched toward where they heard firing still going on and provided Thomas's men with much-needed reinforcement. Bierce himself performed this action, he says; it is no coincidence that he begins his explanation of the battle with the statement that "Chickamauga was not my first battle by many, for although hardly more than a boy in years, I had served at the front from the beginning of the trouble, and had seen enough of war to give me a fair understanding of it" (32). He had seen enough, in fact, to know not only that moving toward the sound of the guns was the correct action but also that doing so had nothing to do with illusions such as heroism, being instead simply the most logical alternative. "A good deal of nonsense," Bierce explains,

> used to be talked about the heroism of General Garfield, who, caught in the rout of the right, nevertheless went back and joined the undefeated left under General Thomas. There was no great heroism in it; that is what every man should have done, including the commander of the army. We could hear Thomas's guns going—those of us who had ears for them—and all that was needful was to make a sufficiently wide detour and then move toward the sound. I did so myself, and have never thought that it ought to make me President. (35)[7]

This proto-existentialist notion of marching toward the sound of the guns brings me back to the starting point of my study of Bierce, for in a certain respect it can provide an explanation for the issue with which this study began, that Bierce's war writing, unlike De Forest's, reveals very little influence from other writers. That De Forest should regard certain kinds of combat writing favorably enough to emulate them makes considerable sense, given that at the time he first saw combat he was already an established writer in his mid-thirties; for him no experience was so dreadful that it could not be encompassed within the perspective of his own broad reading and his writerly desire to make sense on paper of what he had been through—even if to do so he had to blink, as he himself admitted, at "the extreme horror of battle." Bierce, on the other hand, came to war an unformed youth of eighteen, and it is likely that combat impressed itself so intensely on the tabula rasa of his adolescent mind that nothing he had read previously about battle prepared him for it and nothing he read afterward matched the nature and intensity of his memories. In the nearly twenty years between his service in the Civil War and the time he began writing about it, Bierce had ample opportunity to consider any number of possible models for his own work, and, as his newspaper commentary makes clear, he read a great deal of war writing and found all of it wanting. Given these facts, it seems just slightly inaccurate to say, as Solomon and Ziff hypothesize, that Bierce had no influences upon his combat writing. Rather, he seems to have had many negative ones; in other words, he transcends his models not in De Forest's manner of rejecting many and blending a few, but by rejecting all and forging a vision of combat entirely his own.[8] While De Forest sees himself as part of the historical continuum of worthwhile military writing, for Bierce the only worthwhile military writing is that which eschews all previous military writing as an inevitable source of dangerous illusions. No less as a writer than as a soldier, Bierce refuses all such illusions, and in so doing creates a body of work that for the first time in American literary history does not to the slightest extent gloss over the physical and psychological terrors of battle. Discarding all possible preconceptions about what realistic combat writing is, Bierce simply writes as he marched—toward the sound of the guns.

CONCLUSION

"I Would Not Have Missed This for Any Consideration"

With the close of the previous chapter, I have met the goal I set forth at the beginning of this study, to compare De Forest's and Bierce's combat writings to historical analogues and to each other to explore how and why these two writers derived different "truths" from the same set of verifiable facts. By way of conclusion, I will address two smaller goals that proceed from this work. The first of these is a comparison of those two truths themselves, an inquiry into whether we in our own day might find one more persuasive than the other in light of the large body of war literature and literary criticism that has accumulated in the century and more since De Forest and Bierce gave them expression. The second is a response to charges that both these writers' truths are ultimately not persuasive because their works do not consistently take an antiwar position.

As I noted in the preceding chapter, both De Forest and Bierce arrive at essentially the same stance in response to war. If, as Mary E. Grenander argues, a man discovers who he is through his endurance of the anguish of combat, what De Forest and Bierce themselves and the worthiest of their characters discover is that they are professional soldiers—that is, men who retain their composure under fire through a concentration on the immediate practical demands they face in that situation. Nevertheless, as I also noted, at another level, that of the means by which they reach this discovery—De Forest via the traditions of duty and honor passed down in military history, Bierce via his own version of existentialism—they seem diametrically opposed, with De Forest arguing that honestly written history can make battle intellectually and emotionally manageable for its participants and Bierce contending that no such history is possible because combat is an ahistorical nightmare that every man must confront anew.

This opposition seems to make a comparative judgment of the persuasiveness of De Forest's and Bierce's insights inevitable, and on the whole this comparison appears to favor Bierce. Certainly De Forest's own comment to Howells that he distorted his picture of battle by deemphasizing its horror and fear gives credence to the argument that his depiction is deficient when placed alongside Bierce's, in which these elements are ever-present. In response to such a judgment one might once again bring up De Forest's point that any rendition of life is necessarily only a selection of facts and buttress that assertion with Stephen Becker's comment concerning *Miss Ravenel's Conversion* that "[a]lways, even when realism predominates overwhelmingly, good novelists distort, rather than report, real life, their own experience, to weave literal and accurate tapestries" (28). One might also cite Andrew Rutherford's dictum, concerning war literature in general, that

> [i]n the last resort we want an author's valuation of war experience to be based on recognizable, authentic, convincing renderings of that experience: otherwise the fictional validation is suspect. . . . [But on] a more sophisticated level it must obviously be conceded that an artist's right to select from the infinity of life's phenomena implies also the right to reject; that his right to shape into significance implies a right to distort; that his right to interpret implies a right to falsify what the historian would see as truth. (197)

Following this line of contention, one could conclude that De Forest's and Bierce's disparate visions are, as De Forest himself said concerning the dissimilar products of different kinds of artists, "equally allowable and in a certain sense equally true," being simply the different products of two diverse temperaments responding to the same events, and, as such, simply evidence of the multiplex nature of truth.

This argument, however, appears to run aground on a caveat with which Rutherford follows the assertions quoted above. The artist's rights to distort and falsify the historical truth in the service of artistic significance, he says, "should be exercised with caution by the war novelist. The kind of lies an artist can tell successfully to make us realize truth depends partly on the knowledge and assumptions of his audience, partly on the nature and conventions of the genre in which he is working" (197).

The knowledge and assumptions of a modern American audience of engaged readers, as well as their understanding of the nature and conventions of the genre of the war story, are derived largely from the literature of the Vietnam War, including the reportage and fiction of Michael Herr, Gustav Hasford, and Tim O'Brien, as well as the films of Francis Ford Coppola, Stanley Kubrick, and Oliver Stone, to name just a few examples. Given this intellectual and aesthetic background, a modern audience would seem likely to accept as both accurate and true Bierce's explicitly subjective, hallucinatory representations, in which conventional, traditional ideals of honor and duty are the paths to despair and death, and concomitantly to reject De Forest's largely impersonal, calmly straightforward depictions, with their implicit message that in their emphasis on duty and honor they provide models for future combatants. O'Brien's assessment of the nature and conventions of the war story in *The Things They Carried* sharply illustrates one of the potential problems with De Forest's work when considered from a contemporary perspective. Given his condemnation of Tacitus for moralizing in his war reports whereas Caesar does not, De Forest would likely agree with O'Brien's narrator's basic statement that a "true war story is never moral." However, he would probably disagree with the details of the later writer's development of this point: "It does not instruct, nor encourage virtue, nor suggest models of proper human behavior, nor restrain men from doing the things men have always done. If a story seems moral, do not believe it. If at the end of a war story you feel uplifted, or if you feel that some small bit of rectitude has been salvaged from the larger waste, then you have been made the victim of a very old and terrible lie" (76).

With these considerations in view, what we would seem to have in De Forest's and Bierce's work is not two truths but one falsehood and one truth. De Forest's falsehood can be explained as the result of a sensibility that remained inescapably a product of its times. At his best, in *Miss Ravenel's Conversion,* De Forest can be regarded as a pioneering but ultimately limited realist, a "protorealist," in John Limon's phrase (37), who, however much he desired to tell the whole truth as he saw it, could not break completely free from either the romantic literary conventions or the traditional conception of military professionalism prevailing in his era. Just as he could not resist educating Lillie Ravenel about the historical rightness of the North's cause through his romance plot, so he could not resist making even his unquestionably factually accurate war scenes equally if more quietly point a moral (a criticism that could also be applied to his memoirs)—could not resist excessively falsifying the effects of fear and the force of duty and honor in his desire to have these scenes explain, in his own words, not only "just what war is" but also "what to do amidst its difficulties and perplexities" ("Military Past" 572), and, not coincidentally, to have them ratify his own professionalism as a soldier-writer. Conversely, Bierce's truth can be accounted for as the logical product of his more intense, idiosyncratic, iconoclastic temper, of his contempt for literary and military conventions of any sort, traits that have impelled critics continually to consider him a strikingly modern figure, to regard him variously as an existentialist, a nihilist, and even, in Cathy Davidson's insightful and elegant work, a deconstructionist.

However, this judgment is finally too simple, neater than the whole range of the facts will allow. Despite his contradiction of our conventional contemporary view, De Forest should not be dismissed, for what emerges from much of the combat literature of all eras is a sense that war is so immense and intense an experience that contradiction is the largest "truth" of all. Wondering how to generalize about war in the course of his meditation on true war stories, O'Brien notes, "War is hell, but that's not the half of it, because war is also mystery and terror and adventure and courage and discovery and holiness and pity and despair and longing and love. War is nasty; war is fun. War is thrilling; war is drudgery. War makes you a man; war makes you dead. . . . To generalize about war is like generalizing about peace. Almost everything is true. Almost nothing is true" (86–87).

As if to confirm this point, in an interview O'Brien talks about the moral dimension of war stories in a way that seems to qualify if not contradict what he says in *The Things They Carried* about such stories' not offering useful models of human behavior. Among the functions of war stories, he says, "is the moral function, which [of course] . . . is not just for war stories. All stories have at their heart an essential moral function, which isn't only to put yourself into someone's shoes, but to go beyond that and put yourself into someone else's moral framework. How would you behave in that world? What is the moral thing to do and not to do?" (McNerney 10).

As though he were thinking specifically of De Forest's depiction of Colburne's dilemma in the assault on Port Hudson, when he decides on the basis of the Army Regulations to enjoin his men from dropping out of ranks to help their wounded comrades, O'Brien then poses this example: "What would *you* do if you were a company commander and knew you had to try to win a war, but also preserve your men? Sometimes you can't preserve your men and win a war. How are you going to make the moral judgments? How would you behave in this or that world?" (McNerney 10). Perhaps, given the complexity of this question and the contradictory reality of war, the wisest course is to allow the "truth" of both De Forest and Bierce; perhaps we should not suppress one voice in favor of the other but let the dialogic combination of the two voices tell us more about the paradoxes of combat than either one can do alone.

The second point I wish to address also concerns the issues of contemporary norms of judgment and contradictory voices. A criticism that has been frequently leveled at Civil War veterans' writings in general is that they are not worthy of serious consideration because the authors treat war with ambivalence, because they do not regard it as something wholly abhorrent. David Lundberg provides one fairly recent version of this condemnation, writing in 1984 that

> [t]he literary realists . . . , men like John De Forest, Ambrose Bierce, and Stephen Crane, do offer a grim and horrifying view of the Civil

> War. Yet they do so not for any pacifistic reason. . . . [T]he realists' vivid descriptions of combat were meant to enhance the status of those who endured the fighting, not condemn the war or the violence that accompanied it. For them . . . war represented the ultimate test of manhood; it was something terrible and frightening but still a means of proving one's worth. . . . [Civil War] veterans looked back on their war years with fondness, remembering them as a time of unity, idealism, and dedication. (376)

Regarding the content of the material in question, Lundberg is correct on both counts. We have seen that De Forest and Bierce both provide horror and suffering in plenty. *Miss Ravenel's Conversion* ends with one of its two military protagonists—Colonel Carter—dead, and the other—Captain Colburne—broken in health, as De Forest himself was by 1864. Bierce's stories almost invariably conclude with the protagonist dead; Bierce presumably counted himself one of the lucky ones to have emerged badly wounded. Yet there is also no denying Lundberg's assertion that for these men war is not completely worthless, for in several instances they reveal fond memories, if not of idealism exactly, at least of manhood, unity, and dedication. Bierce's nostalgia is clearest in the late story "A Resumed Identity." As discussed in the preceding chapter, the protagonist of this story, who bears a close resemblance to Bierce himself, finds a visit to the field of Stone River fifty years after the battle so affecting that he loses all consciousness of his intervening life and imagines himself once again a part of the army that bled on this spot. When he is disabused of this notion, he pitches forward and dies. Also significant in this respect is the fact that the final act of Bierce's life was his 1913 journey to Mexico to observe or perhaps even participate in another war, and that this journey was preceded by a well-publicized tour of the Civil War battlefields that held a place in his memory. Perhaps the most telling piece of evidence of all is the melancholy interview with a reporter for the *New Orleans State* that Bierce gave during this tour, in the course of which he remarked that he did not believe he "'had amounted to much'" since his Civil War service (qtd. in O'Connor 301).

A similar note sounds in one passage in *Miss Ravenel's Conversion*. De Forest here does not spare the reader nauseating terrors in visions of the battle line, the battlefield surgical station—with its piles of amputated limbs in pools of blood under tables—and the hospitals behind the lines. And in *A Volunteer's Adventures* he says that "[c]ertain military authors who never heard a bullet whistle have written copiously . . . to the general effect that fighting is delightful. It is not; it is just tolerable; you can put up with it; but you can't honestly praise it" (123). Nevertheless, his depiction of Colburne's courage and skill in repelling the Confederate attack on Fort Winthrop prompts him to wax briefly nostalgic, although he is careful to qualify this impulse as one of the heart's more peculiar products. "Such was the defense of Fort Winthrop," he says,

> one of the most gallant feats of the war. Those days are gone by, and there will be no more like them forever, at least not in our forever. Not very long ago, no more than two hours before this ink dried upon the paper, the author of the present history was sitting on the edge of a basaltic cliff which overlooked a wide expanse of fertile earth, flourishing villages, the spires of a city, and, beyond, a shining sea flecked with the full-blown sails of peace and prosperity. From the face of another basaltic cliff two miles distant, he saw a white globule of smoke dart a little way upward, and a minute afterwards heard a dull, deep *pum!* of exploding gunpowder. Quarrymen there were blasting out rocks from which to build hives of industry and happy family homes. But the sound reminded him of the roar of artillery; of the thunder of those signal guns which used to presage battle; of the alarums which only a few months previous were a command to him to mount and ride into the combat. Then he thought almost with a feeling of sadness, so strange is the human heart, that he had probably heard those clamors uttered in mortal earnest for the last time. Never again, perhaps, even should he live to the age of threescore and ten, would the shriek of grape-shot, and the crash of shell, and the multitudinous whiz of musketry be a part of his life. Nevermore would he hearken to that charging yell which once had stirred his blood more fiercely than the sound of trumpets: the Southern battle-yell, full of howls and yelpings as of brute beasts rushing hilariously to the fray: the long-sustained Northern yell, all human, but none the less relentless and stern; nevermore the one nor the other. No more charges of

cavalry, rushing through the dust of the distance; no more answering smoke of musketry, veiling unshaken lines and squares; no more columns of smoke, piling high above deafening batteries. No more groans of wounded, nor shouts of victors over positions carried and banners captured, nor reports of triumphs which saved a nation from disappearing off the face of the earth. After thinking of these things for an hour together, almost sadly, as I have said, he walked back to his home; and read with interest a paper which prattled of town elections and advertised corner lots for sale; and decided to make a kid-gloved call in the evening and to go to church on the morrow. (319–20)

Given the presence of this sentiment in both De Forest's and Bierce's works, Lundberg cannot be faulted for finding these authors not entirely pacifistic. But it is a mistake to dismiss such works on the basis of this sentiment. In fact, this ambivalence may make these works more realistic, more truthful, than the wholly antimartial World War I and World War II novels that Lundberg values more highly, since such ambivalence is characteristic of many veterans of all wars. While some survivors do take a wholly antiwar stance, Richard Holmes's exhaustive studies suggest that most regard war—even modern, mechanized, impersonal war—not altogether unfavorably concerning their manhood and senses of unity and dedication. With regard to a vision of war as the ultimate test of the veteran's manhood, Holmes reports that a "feeling of having grown up as a result of war is almost universal" (396). He cites, among others, an Israeli paratrooper who says, "'I'll tell you in two words what . . . battle was. . . . Murder and fear, murder and fear. . . . [But] I know I'll never be the same person again. . . . All the things that used to bother me are so small and silly. I know what life is worth, now I've seen so much death'" (396).

Similarly, Wilfred Owen, who can scarcely be criticized for blindness to the horrors of war, believed that it helped him grow up. Writing to his mother from the western front on 8 August 1917, he says,

> The other day I read a biography of Tennyson, which says he was unhappy, even in the midst of his fame, wealth, and domestic serenity. Divine discontent! I can quite believe he never knew happiness for one moment such as I have—for one or two moments. But as for

misery, was he ever frozen alive, with dead men for comforters. Did he hear the moaning at the bar, not at twilight and the evening bell only, but at dawn, noon, and night, eating and sleeping, walking and working, always the close moaning of the Bar; the thunder, the hissing and the whining of the Bar?

Tennyson, it seems, was always a great child.

So should I have been, but for Beaumont Hamel [the sector of the western front in which Owen first took part in combat, in January 1917]. (*Collected Letters* 482)

As O'Brien says, "War makes you a man; war makes you dead."

A bittersweet sense that, for all its carnage, war promotes an unparalleled bond among its participants, along with glimmerings of dedication to a higher purpose, is also common. Holmes quotes an Australian veteran of the Falklands War on this point:

One is jolly glad to be out of it, yet . . . men you have been friendly with and stood side by side with for months or perhaps into years . . . have been killed—one's heart fills with sadness—and one has a hankering to be back over there with "the boys" once more. Whatever one may be in private life, when you are in the line facing the same enemies, fear, death and other horrors, you are absolutely one, and one gets momentary glimpses of that truer and greater democracy which is gradually opening out to solve all human problems. (397)

Even the Vietnam War, widely regarded as one of the most ferociously absurd wars in history, occasionally engenders such feelings. "'Thinking about Vietnam,'" one veteran said to Holmes, "'once in a while, in a crazy kind of way, I wish that just for an hour I could be there. And then be transported back. Maybe just be there so I'd wish I was back here again'" (403). In the same vein, O'Brien's narrator in *The Things They Carried* says that he was delighted when his combat rotation ended, but "[i]n an odd way, . . . there were times when I missed the adventure, even the danger, of the real war out in the boonies. It's a hard thing to explain to somebody who hasn't felt it, but the presence of death and danger has a way of bringing you fully awake. . . . When you're afraid, really afraid, you see things you never saw before, you pay attention to the world. You make close friends. You become part of a tribe and you share the same blood—you give it together, you take it together" (219–20).

Perhaps, then, De Forest and Bierce should not be judged too harshly for voicing similar sentiments. Perhaps, in fact, the final word should go to a Civil War veteran who perfectly captures this ambivalence, in terms that a critic who has never heard a bullet whistle (I refer to myself) should bear carefully in mind. "'War is hell broke loose and benumbs all the tender feelings of men and makes of them brutes,'" writes Sergeant Cyrus Boyd of the Fifteenth Iowa Infantry. "'I do not want to see any more such scenes and yet I would not have missed this for any consideration'" (qtd. in Robertson 227).

Notes

Introduction

1. Although Whitman was not a veteran in the strict sense of the term, his service to the wounded in Union hospitals gave him considerable insight into the reality of war, as his wartime entries in *Specimen Days* attest. He himself makes this point most explicitly in the same entry in which he asserts that the real war will not find its way into books. The hospitals, he says, were where "the marrow of the tragedy [was] concentrated," so much so that "it seem'd sometimes as if the whole interest of the land, North and South, was one vast central hospital, and all the rest of the affair but flanges" (113). The accuracy of Whitman's understanding of "the real war" will be borne out later in this study, in the section on Bierce.
2. All told, at least forty Civil War veterans wrote novels and stories that prominently feature the war, and most of these are assessed in Robert A. Lively's *Fiction Fights the Civil War,* Edmund Wilson's *Patriotic Gore,* Wayne Charles Miller's *Armed America,* Daniel Aaron's *Unwritten War,* David Madden and Peggy Bach's introduction to *Classics of Civil War Fiction,* and John A. Limon's *Writing After War.* All these critics agree that the majority of these works are, in Miller's words, little more than "romantic tales spiced with sectional vituperation (54). As Lively points out, "Battle experience . . . was no guarantee of real-

istic detail. . . . For every ex-soldier . . . whose stories of . . . campaigns included accurate memoirs of real battles and leaders, there are two more who follow the pattern of George Cary Eggleston, whose romances are but lightly touched with war realities" (30). Miller argues that, aside from De Forest and Bierce, only two other veteran-authors make sustained efforts to get close to "the way it was": Kirkland, a former Union officer, and former Confederate Lanier.

3. Keegan notes that the writer who did the most to popularize this style in the nineteenth century was not Napier but the English historian Sir Edward Creasy. Creasy's 1851 *Fifteen Decisive Battles of the World* was one of the great Victorian best sellers in England and America and spawned a great many similar volumes in both countries (57).

Chapter 1. What the Soldier Does in Combat

1. Eric Solomon notes just such a lack of concern with the issues over which the war was fought in battle scenes in Civil War fiction, but he offers an explanation that differs from Dollard's. His view is that because this war was a sectional conflict rather than an international one the combatants did not truly hate one another and thus did not develop the kind of intense devotion to their own cause and hatred for the enemy's that obtains in most wars (Introduction viii). More recently, James McPherson, in *For Cause and Comrades*, has found, based on the writings of many Civil War soldiers, that many soldiers on both sides enlisted and remained in service for reasons of patriotism, sectional ideology, religion, and personal duty and honor (21–24). However, most also reported that in the heat of combat they fought simply to stay alive and, if they were officers, they focused on efficiently directing the men for whom they were immediately responsible (39). This latter motivation, as well as others that McPherson mentions, including the feeling that cowardice was shameful (77–81) and a strong sense of cohesion with one's fellow combatants (85–86), are also central in the writings of Dollard, S. L. A. Marshall, and many other writers on combat psychology. They will be discussed in chapter 2.

2. Despite these facts and figures, Civil War tactics never changed entirely from mass to loose formations. In *The Battle Cry of Freedom*, James McPherson explains the lack of total transition: "as time went on experience taught soldiers new tactics adapted to the rifle. Infantry formations loosened up and became a sort of large-scale skirmish line in which men advanced by rushes, taking advantage of cover offered by the ground to reload before dashing forward another few yards, working in groups of two or three to load and shoot alternately in order to keep up a continuous rather than a volley fire. But officers had difficulty maintaining control over large units employing such tactics in that pre-radio age. This limited the employment of loose-order tactics and compelled the retention of close-order assaults in some instances to the end of the war" (475–

76). Such assaults did remain relatively rare, however; McPherson notes that "one of the war's few genuine bayonet charges" (644)—and one of the even fewer successful ones—occurred on 3 May 1863. While the bulk of General Joseph Hooker's Union Army of the Potomac engaged Lee's Confederates at Chancellorsville, Hooker ordered General John Sedgwick's detached Sixth Corps to seize Confederate entrenchments at Fredericksburg, nine miles away, in an attempt to get behind Lee's main body. In three mass assaults with fixed bayonets, Sedgwick's troops accomplished this objective.

Chapter 2. What the Soldier Feels in Combat

1. Although some military historians have questioned certain of Marshall's methods and findings, as summarized in a 1989 article by Fredric Smoler for *American Heritage,* no one has disputed the continued presence of fear in the soldier's makeup and the procedure by which the soldier copes with it. As this chapter bears out, most other historians are in close agreement.

Chapter 3. The Soldier's Experience in De Forest and Bierce

1. A broader contemporary version of this statement comes from the first volume of William James's *Principles of Psychology:* "Men have no eyes but for those aspects of things which they have already been taught to discern" (127). For examples of American soldiers' grapplings with this condition, see *The Written Wars,* edited by Joseph T. Cox, which seeks discussion on several questions with which I am concerned: "How do Americans construct coherent representations out of the often incomprehensible realities of war? What are the rhetorical techniques they employ? What are the consequences of the social myths that result from the constructions of American justifications of war and warmaking?" (xiii).

Chapter 4. The Limits of Experience

1. Most critics take the approach of the contemporary reviewer for the *Nation,* who passes lightly over the novel's romance plot and says that "it is as a picture of the military service . . . that we think best of the book" (2). William Dean Howells takes this tack in the *Atlantic Monthly,* focusing his praise on the fact that "Mr. De Forest is the first to treat the war realistically and artistically" (120). The anonymous critics for *Harper's Monthly* and the *New York Post* note respectively that the novel "contains some capital battle pieces, admirably done" (401), and that the battle scenes are "done with great spirit" (1). (I am indebted to James W. Gargano for his lists of contemporary reviews of *Miss Ravenel's Conversion* in his article "John W. De Forest and the Critics" and his introduction to *Critical Essays on John William De Forest.*)

More recently but in the same vein, Alexander Cowie criticizes De Forest for his "leisurely, almost negligent" narrative style, but he also notes that "[f]or the first time in the history of the American novel, war is treated with steady realism and quiet honesty" (508). Harold Kolb finds little to admire in the "leisurely comedy of manners" of the sections of the book that deal with the society of New Boston, the New England college town—De Forest's thin disguise for his own hometown, New Haven—in which the story begins and ends, but he praises De Forest's "sharp and vivid scenic portrayals of the dusty horrors of the battlefield" (139). More generally, James A. Hijiya asserts that the novel "contain[s] . . . some very feeble passages" but also, in its depictions of combat, "much of the strongest writing De Forest would ever do" (92).

Even most of those critics who find the novel irreparably flawed by the melodrama of the romance plot concede its power as a realistic depiction of war. Eric Solomon argues that *Miss Ravenel's Conversion* epitomizes the condition of the American war novel in the 1860s and 1870s: whereas European writers such as de Vigny, Stendhal, Zola, and Tolstoy had by this time developed a "tradition of irony and realism" in war fiction, their American counterparts lagged behind, writing romances in which war served essentially as a backdrop "for a stirring love story often complicated by the Northern versus Southern brother theme" (*Parody* 70). While *Miss Ravenel's Conversion from Secession to Loyalty* substitutes for the warring brothers theme the titular alteration in Lillie's feelings from Southern to Northern sympathies, largely as a result of Colburne's devotion, its love story, Solomon notes, is still unalterably romantic, drawn from Walter Scott and Thackeray, most markedly from *Vanity Fair* (*Parody* 72). Nevertheless, Solomon asserts in a separate study that the central factor in determining the worth of a war novel is its combat scenes, since these depict "the ultimate pressure, the extreme stress, the essential test" (*Banners* viii), and in this area he finds De Forest worthy of considerable praise; the novel ultimately fails not because of a lack of realism where war is concerned, but due to the discrepancy, the lack of integration, between its powerful depictions of battle and its derivative, pedestrian handling of romance (*Parody* 72).

Likewise, Stephen Becker acknowledges that De Forest "was no Stendhal or Tolstoy," not a master of the form of the war novel, because "his episodes are less integrated, the flow meanders . . . [and] his characters . . . betray somewhat of their descent from literature's earlier 'humors,'" but he nevertheless rates him highly as "the first American to write realistically and grimly of war from first-hand experience" (28). John Limon argues more strenuously that, because of its primary focus on Lillie Ravenel's "conversion" from Southern to Northern sympathies, through the offices of her father, a college professor, and her observation of Colburne's quiet courage in devotion to the North's war aims, the novel is unequivocally a romance; critics have defined it as realistic, he contends, by an excess of attention to the battle scenes. Nevertheless, he concedes that De Forest is "the only combatant to write a realistic novel in the Howellsian mode" (79).

A number of other modern critics are less stinting with their praise; seemingly taking their cue from Solomon's assertion that battle scenes are the central measure of the worth of a war novel, they draw attention only to De Forest's command of the details of warfare and to his uniqueness in this respect compared to his contemporaries. Ernest Leisy, pointing out that *Miss Ravenel's Conversion* "is thoroughly informed about the attitudes of both sides, the official delays, the effect of army maneuvers on noncombatants, and the actual feelings of men in battle," terms it "the one novel of [its] decade that is still readable" (156–57), an opinion Lawrence Thompson shares, praising De Forest's "tough, realistic style," which makes the book the "[o]nly . . . Civil War novel with a secure niche in the history of American literature [that] came out of the Sixties" (85). Edmund Wilson in his landmark study of Civil War literature, *Patriotic Gore*, declares that "the war scenes in *Miss Ravenel's Conversion* were the first of their kind in English, and it would be more than a decade . . . before any other writer of talent who had taken an active part in the war would describe [the war] with equal realism" (685). Citing the inclusion of the "[d]etails of the army camp, soldiers with uniforms dirty from sleeping on the ground and marching through mud and dust many days without washing, the horrible scenes of the battlefield and the scarcely less horrible scenes of the temporary hospitals," Floyd Stovall says that De Forest's novel "pictures the realities of war more faithfully than any other work of fiction before Crane's *Red Badge of Courage*" (372).

2. The importance of such accurate preparedness for combat is De Forest's principal theme in all his nonfiction military writing. In a May 1880 *Atlantic Monthly* review of Loyall Farragut's biography of his Civil War hero father, Admiral David Farragut, De Forest attributes the admiral's success to personal courage and "zeal of preparation": "All his life he both toiled conscientiously in his profession and studied it enthusiastically, seeking not only to do perfectly the duty of the moment, but also to fit himself for every supposable emergency" (689). Similarly, in "Caesar's Art of War and of Writing," De Forest emphasizes that "with all Caesar's swiftness and artfulness, there was no lack of forethought, no defect of preparation. The Commentaries show us that his warfare was scientific throughout, and that the means to carry it on were carefully calculated beforehand" (280).

3. In fact, De Forest's call for acquainting prospective soldiers with combat's realities itself closely matches later demands by historians, psychologists, and even other novelists. In *Men Against Fire*, written in 1946, S. L. A. Marshall is as concerned with the harm ignorant romancers can do as De Forest was in 1879. The recruit, Marshall says, "needs to be taught the nature of [the] field as it is in war and as he may experience it some day. For if he does not acquire a soldier's view of the field, his image of it will be formed from the reading of novels or the romance written by war correspondents, or from viewing the battlefield as it is imagined to be by Hollywood. One of the purposes of training should be to remove these false ideas

of battle from his mind" (36). And in 1990 Tim O'Brien likewise raises this issue in *The Things They Carried,* a book of short stories loosely based on his own experiences in Vietnam. In moments of stress in a combat zone, O'Brien says, "[y]ou wonder if you're dreaming. It's like you're in a movie. There's a camera on you, so you begin acting, you're somebody else. You think of all the films you've seen, Audie Murphy and Gary Cooper and the Cisco Kid, all those heroes, and you can't help falling back on them as models of proper comportment" (233).

4. Although most of the material in this volume was published in *Harper's New Monthly Magazine* or *Galaxy* between 1864 and 1868, the book was not published until 1946, edited by James H. Croushore. As Croushore explains in his preface, sometime before 1890 De Forest set out to produce a complete record of his military service, revising these magazine articles and drawing on a number of letters he had written to his wife during this period to fill in the gaps. However, this manuscript, which he had entitled *Military Life,* remained unpublished at his death in 1906 (xii).

5. This and all the ensuing quotations from "The First Time Under Fire" are from the version printed in *Harper's,* which is somewhat more expansive than the one included in *A Volunteer's Adventures.*

6. Creasy's source for asserting that this speech passed through the Greek ranks at Salamis, a naval victory over the Persians in 480 B.C., is Aeschylus, who, as Creasy points out (35), served in the Greek force both in this engagement and at Marathon.

7. Weitzel's businesslike attitude in this instance notwithstanding, high-flown addresses to the troops were not at all uncommon during the Civil War; very probably influenced by their own reading of Creasy and other authors of conventional "battle-pieces," many commanders eagerly seized the moments just before or after battle to indulge in high-flown speeches. The War Department's *Official Records of the Union and Confederate Armies* reports that on the eve of the battle of Shiloh, Confederate General Albert Sidney Johnston told his assembled forces, "[T]he eyes and hopes of eight millions of people rest upon you. You are expected to show yourselves worthy of your race and lineage; worthy of the women of the South, whose noble devotion in this war has never been exceeded at any time. With such incentives to brave deeds and with the trust that God is with us, your general will lead you confidently to the combat, assured of success" (qtd. in Robertson, *Soldiers* 215).

Chapter 5. The Uses of Influence

1. Keegan arrives at his conclusion of Caesar's primacy of influence on the battle-piece by textual induction rather than historical deduction. One might, Keegan says, laboriously construct a case by beginning with the well-documented fact that the

Romans in general and Caesar in particular provided the models for most armies in the period immediately following the Renaissance and from this fact conclude that Caesar must have had a concomitant influence on post-Renaissance military writing. Keegan asserts, however, that "[w]e can reach the same point by a single inductive leap, for the distinctive features of the 'battle piece' will all be found in any of Caesar's narratives of his own victories that one cares to turn up" (64–65).

2. It is possible that in Colburne's comments De Forest has in mind Plutarch's account of this battle, which appears in Pompey's biography in *The Lives*. A reference to Caesar's work is more likely, however, in that Caesar reports the casualty figures De Forest mentions—two hundred of Caesar's men killed as opposed to fifteen thousand of Pompey's (325–26)—whereas Plutarch revises the figure for Pompey's losses to six thousand (534). But even if De Forest is specifically taking Plutarch to task here rather than Caesar, the ultimate blame still rests with Caesar, as De Forest doubtless knew; being familiar with both accounts, he would have been aware that Plutarch closely follows the *Commentaries*' report of this battle.

3. Although Kinglake has today been largely forgotten, in the late nineteenth and early twentieth centuries many writers and critics rated him highly as a historian and stylist. Both Rudyard Kipling and Winston Churchill acknowledged his work as a major influence on their own battle writing (Bocca 17–18, 24).

4. In October 1864 De Forest was promoted from his command of a company in the Twelfth Connecticut to the staff of Brevet Major General William H. Emory, the commander of the Nineteenth Army Corps, of which the Twelfth Connecticut formed a part. Much of De Forest's responsibility in this post was to write accounts of this corps for publication, an assignment resulting from the favorable impression his earlier magazine articles about his war experiences had made on his superiors. According to James H. Croushore, the writing De Forest produced in this new role differs markedly from his earlier memoirs. "Since [De Forest's] new post enabled him to observe the broad strategy of various engagements," Croushore says, "the final part of *A Volunteer's Adventures* lost the tone of personal narrative and assumed more and more that of military history" (191), by which Croushore presumably means the kind of history told from a commander's-eye view, the kind of history for which Caesar's *Commentaries* is one of the original models. But even in the accounts to which Croushore refers, which chiefly cover Sheridan's Shenandoah Valley campaign, De Forest is careful to explain the roles company-level officers and private soldiers play as well as those played by corps commanders; the mixture of the broad strategic picture with individuals' actions is in fact not markedly different from De Forest's handling of the battle of Labadieville in the earlier "First Time Under Fire." During his description of the battle of Cedar Creek,

for instance, De Forest provides the large contours of the battle's action—the movements of brigades and corps and the like—but he also shifts frequently to the personal level, as in his noting that at one point during a charge by his old regiment, "[h]ere and there the antagonists were so intermingled that they held hasty martial dialogues. Charles Wells of my [former] company, being summoned to surrender by three Southerners, instantly shot one of them, and was shot by the two others. Lieutenant Mullen . . . called to a squad which he supposed to belong to the Eighth Vermont, 'What the devil are you firing this way [i.e., toward Mullen] for?' The answer was, 'Surrender, you d——d Yankee!' followed by more shooting, too hasty to be effective. . . . Lieutenant Colonel Lewis, the commander of the Twelfth, got away by galloping past a swarm of Rebels and through a shower of bullets amid cries of 'Kill that officer!'" (212).

5. Stone regards De Forest's pared-down style as "one of his signal contributions to American literature. . . . If a major problem for the modern writer has been to devise ways to purify language of inherited abuses, here is an early forerunner of Crane and Hemingway who has done just that" (87).

6. For a full discussion of the obstacles to promotion De Forest faced and his vain efforts to surmount them, see James A. Hijiya, *J. W. De Forest and the Rise of American Gentility,* 56–58.

7. De Forest's connection of Caesar's style to his innate gentility ("[n]othing could be more high bred, more thoroughly like the speech of a finished gentleman" [288]) in addition to his military prowess is likely also important in De Forest's desire to adopt this style for himself. As James A. Hijiya has persuasively argued, the concept of the gentleman, "a man of uncommon refinement—of good breeding and high ideals—but also a man of strength—of daring and courage and force" (2), is one of the central themes in De Forest's work. Perhaps corroborating this view is De Forest's one attempt in "Caesar's Art of War and of Writing" to account for Caesar's general sketchiness about the hows and whys of his battles' outcomes; he asserts that this quality derives from Caesar's understanding of his audience. "Caesar could well be concise," De Forest says, "for he wrote only for the eye of statesmen and soldiers and scholars, men who would comprehend him at a word. Officers and gentlemen did not need long-winded explanations to make them understand military movements . . ." (287).

Chapter 6. The Failures of History

1. Bierce's most expansive comments on another combat writer mentioned by name are his harsh judgments of Stephen Crane. As reported in Stanley Wertheim and Paul Sorrentino's *Crane Log,* a *New York Journal* reviewer named Percival Pollard asserted in a column for 22 May 1896 that *The Red Badge of Courage* was

an inept imitation of Bierce's war stories; Bierce wrote to Pollard on 25 May that he valued this judgment "more for its just censure of the Crane freak than for its too kindly praise of me. I have been hoping someone still in the business of reading (I have not myself looked into a book for months) would take the trouble to say something of that kind about that Crane person's work" (185). In the same vein, the *New York Press* for 25 July 1896 quotes Bierce as saying, "I had thought there could be only two worse writers than Stephen Crane, namely, two Stephen Cranes" (197). Bierce's kindest assessment of Crane's work in *The Red Badge* is what seems to be a backhanded compliment reported by Robert H. Davis: "This young man has the power to feel. He knows nothing of war, yet he is drenched with blood" (qtd. in *Crane Log* 197).

2. In addition to pointing out both authors' general treatment of war as unheroic, Ahnebrink says that the vision of escaping hanging and returning to his family that comes to Peyton Farquhar in the moment before his death in "An Occurrence at Owl Creek Bridge" has its original in a scene in *Sebastopol* in which the central character, Mikhailoff, witnesses scenes from his past life in the instant before a shell explodes almost on top of him. Ahnebrink also points out that in another short story, "One of the Missing," Bierce, "in the manner of Tolstoy [in *War and Peace*], explained the events as the result of a concatenation of a series of circumstances" (352). Given these points, the case here seems to be much the same as that of the influence of Stendhal and Thackeray on De Forest, as discussed in chapter 5: while Bierce may have found Tolstoy's attitude toward war and the individual's consciousness in battle congenial, he did not draw on Tolstoy for specific techniques by which to depict combat realistically.

3. De Forest does not deny that some men succumb to these feelings and crack up, but he describes such failures as exceptions brought on by specific, extraordinary conditions, not as the inevitable results of combat's stresses. In one of his memoirs, "After Port Hudson," for instance, he mentions a lieutenant of his regiment who "wandered about camp with a downcast air, complaining to one and another that people were slandering him" and then vanished, only to be discovered somewhat later, a suicide. Such behavior, De Forest says, is the result of "an insane access of country fever" (153).

4. In this indirect statement of the rarity of bayonet fighting, we see yet another resemblance to De Forest's and the historians' assertions concerning the actualities of combat.

5. O'Connor also notes that H. L. Mencken called Bierce "'the first writer of fiction ever to treat war realistically'" (5). Others who make particular mention of what O'Connor calls Bierce's "startling air of realism" (5) include Larzer Ziff, who says that until Bierce's memoirs and stories appeared "the murderous side of the war was an oral tradition only" (166); Eric Solomon, who asserts that Bierce's

"accumulation of exact, realistic, and factual observations of combat life" creates "the feeling of reality, the sense of fact and place that makes war not an abstract moral condition but a concrete physical actuality" ("Bitterness" 182, 185); and William McCann, who says that in reading Bierce's work "we feel unmistakably that here are men at war" (iv).

6. Because, unlike De Forest's confrontation in "The First Time Under Fire," this is not Bierce's first encounter with a wounded man, it might at first seem logical to ascribe Bierce's vicious humor to a long-developed embitterment, the product of having seen many wounded men and thus having grown callous to the sight. Bierce, however, claims to have felt impelled to this strain of brutal comedy from the beginning of his military career. In a column in the *San Francisco Examiner* of 19 July 1891, Bierce recalls that he first saw a wounded man, Colonel Kelley of the First West Virginia Infantry, in his initial engagement, a skirmish at Philippi, West Virginia. He reports himself as having had much the same cruelly jocose reaction as he evinces at Shiloh. Kelley's wound, Bierce says, was "spang through the breast, a hole that you could have put two fingers in. And, bless my soul! how it bled! Wounds were new to my observation in those golden days, and I said to myself, with Lady Macbeth: 'Who would have thought the old man to have had so much blood in him!'" (qtd. in Fatout 38–39).

7. For discussions of the relative merits of Hood's and Cheatham's claims, see Cox, *Battle of Franklin* and *March to the Sea*; Hay; Hood; McDonough and Connelly; and McMurry.

8. Bierce also takes up the question of Grant's conduct at Shiloh in "What I Saw of Shiloh" and the short story "An Affair of Outposts." Compared to his remarks in his eulogy for Buell, his tone is relatively mild in "What I Saw of Shiloh." He simply notes that in the face of a large Confederate force Grant "established his army, with a river in his rear and two toy steamboats as a means of communication with the east side, whither General Buell with thirty thousand men was moving to join him from Nashville," and lets the understated strategic errors speak for themselves, speculating only that perhaps Grant's impatience for action impelled him to them (13). In "An Affair of Outposts," however, Bierce is even more outspoken than in Buell's obituary, ascribing the Union losses on the battle's first day to Grant's "manifest incompetence" and lamenting that Grant's command was not given to Buell, since the army "had been saved from destruction and capture by Buell's soldierly activity and skill" (174). Dozens of books and articles have examined the controversy between Grant and Buell; among the best-balanced discussions are Sword's, McDonough's, and McFeely's.

9. In all his war literature, Bierce offers only one instance in which skilled, accurate writing regarding military matters receives its just reward. Lamenting in his *Examiner* column for 29 May 1898 that California's Governor Budd demonstrates a preference for political connections over military skill in his appoint-

ments of officers to the volunteer regiments California is raising for the Spanish-American War, Bierce calls attention to Major H. H. Sargent. This man, he says, is not only a West Point graduate and thirteen-year professional soldier but also "America's foremost writer on military affairs" and thus deserves command of one of these regiments. Bierce points out that Sargent's two tactical and strategic studies, *Bonaparte's First Italian Campaign* and *The Campaign of Marengo,* "have made him famous among military students the world over" and that "[n]o greater work regarding the art of war has ever been done, even by Jomini," and yet Sargent languishes in an administrative post rather than receiving a field command (qtd. in *Skepticism* 42). Bierce's efforts to sway Budd in this matter failed, but two months later, in the *Examiner* for 24 July 1898, Bierce had the satisfaction of noting that Sargent had received command of a national regiment. "It is gratifying to know," Bierce writes, "that the abilities of this accomplished officer have been recognized more signally than I had ventured to suggest—by the President, namely: while Governor Budd's favor has descended like a heavenly dove upon the head of Colonel Park Henshaw, of the Canteenth Fraternizers" (qtd. in *Skepticism* 82).

10. Howard's reasons for such an order are obscure. As Bierce's comments regarding the lack of knowledge under which even generals operate in battle emphasize, Howard could not have known how many Confederates opposed his attacking brigade, and he may have intended this assault as a way of finding out the enemy's strength. But in Bierce's eyes the decision to use a single brigade in this situation manifestly demonstrates Howard's lack of military acuity regardless of his motive, for Bierce asserts that any capable officer would have seen that the difficult terrain and the extent of the Confederate entrenchments alone indicated that a force far larger than a brigade was required for any kind of assault. Regarding the Confederates' large numbers, Bierce admits, "True, we did not *know* all this [emphasis added], but if any man on that ground besides Wood and Howard expected a 'walkover' his must have been a singularly hopeful disposition" (42). (General Thomas Wood was the commander of the division to which Hazen's brigade belonged; Bierce indicts him for lacking both the tactical insight and the moral courage to question Howard's order to attack.)

11. Bierce's particularly acute awareness of the fog of ignorance regarding their own and the enemy's positions in which not only line officers but also generals operated during the Civil War may be traced to the post Bierce himself occupied for much of the war, brigade topographical officer. His responsibility in this post was to map for the leaders the terrain through which the troops were passing; thus, he saw firsthand just how little an army's commanders understood about their circumstances. Bierce notes the high value of any information he could glean, which emphasizes the extent of his commanders' customary lack of information, in the short story "George Thurston." This story's narrator is, like

Bierce, a brigade topographical officer, and early in his tale he explains that his duties are so crucial as to be worth the lives of many of those around him. "Whether in camp or on the march, in barracks, in tents, or *en bivouac*," the narrator says, "my duties as topographical engineer kept me working like a beaver—all day in the saddle and half the night at my drawing-table, platting my surveys. It was hazardous work; the nearer to the enemy's lines I could penetrate, the more valuable were my field notes and the resulting maps. It was a business in which the lives of men counted as nothing against the chance of defining a road or sketching a bridge. Whole squadrons of cavalry escort had sometimes to be sent thundering against a powerful infantry outpost in order that the brief time between the charge and the inevitable retreat might be utilized in sounding a ford or determining the point of intersection of two roads. . . . These spirited encounters were observations entered in red" (214–15). It is worth noting that by all accounts Bierce performed these topographical duties most capably. Paul Fatout, in "Ambrose Bierce, Civil War Topographer," says that Bierce received frequent praise in dispatches from his superiors, and he further notes that Bierce's still-extant maps and reports, necessarily produced hastily and with crude instruments, have been judged excellent by modern military topographers (396).

12. These reports, and those of both sides on all other battles, were published by the War Department between 1880 and 1894 under the title *Official Records of the Union and Confederate Armies.*
13. Couser's insights parallel my own readings of a number of Bierce's pieces, including, in addition to "Pickett's Mill," "What I Saw of Shiloh," "A Little of Chickamauga," and "Jupiter Doke, Brigadier-General."
14. We might note yet another difficulty with Johnston's account that Bierce is silent upon here but is implicitly critical of, given his earlier remarks on the handicaps of knowledge under which even generals operate: Johnston likely did not know until he read Union reports long after the battle that the Union troops attacking this position were members of the Fourth Corps.
15. Bierce's cross-referencing approach to writing history here anticipates the method S. L. A. Marshall presents himself as having discovered during World War II. In *Island Victory,* Marshall describes how he and his team of assistants faced the task of accurately recounting the American victory over the Japanese forces holding the Makin Island group in November 1943. Even while the mopping-up fighting was still going on, Marshall says, "we were already thinking of how to write the history of that battle" (1). Sounding much like Whitman in *Specimen Days,* he explains that "[t]here was a general doubt that the tactical confusions of that strange night of combat would ever be clarified. Few of those who were closest to it, including the actual commanders in the battle, knew much more about it than that our men had behaved well in a difficult situation. None knew the relationship of any one combat episode to another. Even in these first

hours after the fight we were already mixing up parts of the story, and as rumor got about over the island, fable was rapidly being substituted for fact" (1). Faced with this situation, however, Marshall possessed an advantage over Whitman: "all of the actors were present, except the killed or badly wounded, and there had not been many of those. The one way to try for the full, detailed truth of battle was to muster the witnesses and see for once whether the small tactical fogs of war were as impenetrable as we had always imagined they were" (1). The discovery Marshall makes is that these fogs are in fact penetrable; after four days of interviewing the troops involved, he says, "we had discovered to our amazement that every fact of the fight was procurable—that the facts lay dormant in the minds of men and officers, waiting to be developed" (1). If Marshall here sounds far more sanguine than Bierce about the possibility of recovering the whole truth through this method of cross-referencing various accounts, it must be borne in mind that Marshall had an advantage over Bierce as well as over Whitman: he questioned the men who actually fought, rather than consulting the self-serving accounts of those who commanded. Marshall notes that "the memory of the average soldier is unusually vivid as to what he has personally heard, seen, felt and done in the battle," and that "he recognizes the dignity of an official inquiry where the one purpose is to find the truth of battle, and he is not likely to exaggerate" (1). Bierce's work makes clear that none of these things can necessarily be said where generals are concerned.

16. Bierce was more specific in another account. In "Ambrose Bierce, Civil War Topographer," Paul Fatout notes that Bierce recalled this battle once more in his *Examiner* column for 30 October 1898, where he says that half of Hazen's brigade of fifteen hundred were casualties, with over one hundred killed outright (395). Neither Bierce himself nor Fatout indicates Bierce's source for these figures, however.

17. Wilt also asserts that Hazen's book was probably the only source outside his own recollections that Bierce relied on in two other memoirs, "What I Saw of Shiloh" and "A Little of Chickamauga"; for his only other memoir of battle, "What Occurred at Franklin," Wilt shows that Bierce drew from several articles in *Century* magazine's four-volume series *Battles and Leaders of the Civil War* (271). (Hazen is silent on this battle because he did not participate in it.)

18. See especially Royster's analysis of the construction of the public persona of Stonewall Jackson on 68–78.

19. The general under Schama's consideration is James Wolfe, the commander of the British army that defeated the French on the Plains of Abraham outside the city of Quebec in 1759, effectively ending the French and Indian War and securing France's North American territories for Britain. The "grandiloquent lie" here is Benjamin West's highly romanticized 1770 painting of Wolfe's death at the end of this battle, which makes the moment much more heroic than do the

eyewitness reports of Wolfe's subordinates, upon which several earlier, more accurate paintings had been based. "Wolfe must not die like a common soldier under a bush," Schama quotes from West's writings. "To move the mind there should be a spectacle presented to raise and warm the mind and all should be proportioned to the highest idea conceived of the Hero.... A mere matter of fact will never produce the effect" (28).

20. Bierce biographer Richard O'Connor identifies the source of this story as the effort of the "vainglorious" Union general Joseph Hooker to claim a victory for himself in one of the engagements of this campaign, when in fact the Confederates facing his force were broken up and routed by a stampede of horses and mules (215). Couser agrees with this identification but argues that Bierce draws many of the other events of Doke's career from Grant's experience. He notes that the story contains several allusions to Grant's campaign against Forts Henry and Donelson early in the war, and he points out that Doke more closely resembles Grant—at least as Bierce regarded him—than Hooker in having his poor generalship steadily rewarded with advancement and in being given a prominent role in the writing of the history of the war (88–92).

21. Evidence that Bierce intends the editor to be cynical rather than simply as credulous as his readers comes from two sources. The first is Bierce's assertion that many of his own letters to the *Warsaw Commercial* criticizing certain generals as incompetents never ran because the editor "suppressed them for the benefit of the incompetents" (qtd. in De Castro 8). The second is his vividly unflattering definition of *editor* in *The Devil's Dictionary,* which characterizes this figure as one who "spills his will along the paper and cuts it off in lengths to suit" while listening obediently to "the voice of the foreman demanding three inches of wit and six lines of religious meditation, or bidding him turn off the wisdom and whack up some pathos" (28).

22. Couser says that such passages demonstrate that "as history (in two senses), the war belonged to its high-ranking officers, who were twice commissioned: once to fight, and once to write, the war" (92).

23. In accordance with Bierce's dictum about even generals' ignorance concerning the enemy, Buxter of course does not know that Doke commands the opposing force; what he says is that, given the undisciplined state of this brigade, it is "apparently without a commander" (255).

24. Couser makes this point as well, and also notes that Bierce's use of dialect in Peyton's testimony "exposes the pretense and pretension of the official prose that precedes it" (96).

25. Although his willingness to overlook Caesar's shortcomings might suggest that De Forest would not question the veracity of history as written by the men who made it, in one place he at least obliquely addresses this issue. Beginning his narrative in *Miss Ravenel's Conversion* of Colburne's ordeal during the siege of

Port Hudson, based closely on De Forest's own experiences in that venture, the narrator says that he will not attempt a comprehensive history of this campaign. In a vein similar to Bierce's in "The Crime at Pickett's Mill," he explains that "[i]t is too early to tell, it is even too early to know, the whole truth concerning the siege. . . . To an honest man, anxious that the world shall not be humbugged, it is a mournful reflection that perhaps the whole truth never will be known to anyone who will dare or care to tell it. We gained a victory there; we took an important step toward the end of the Rebellion; but at what cost, through what means, and by whose merit?" (256).

Beyond the simple admission of history's limitations in this statement, a note of sarcasm similar to Bierce's in "Jupiter Doke" is unmistakable in the final sentence, aimed at those military writers, such as the Union commander at Port Hudson, Nathaniel Banks, who would deem this siege a "victory" and "an important step toward the end of the Rebellion" and concomitantly take credit for it. As De Forest well knew, this siege was essentially a meaningless slaughter. The Confederates had fortified Port Hudson as a defense of the southern approaches to the far more important port of Vicksburg, Mississippi, which lay 150 miles farther up the Mississippi River. Banks led a force up from New Orleans and invested Port Hudson in March 1863 as part of the larger Union effort to isolate and take Vicksburg. Failing to starve the Confederates out, he launched frontal assaults on 27 May and 14 June, both of which were repulsed with heavy casualties. Banks then settled down to a siege that produced no results but further casualties; Port Hudson only surrendered, on 9 July 1863, because Vicksburg had surrendered to Ulysses S. Grant's army six days earlier, rendering further resistance pointless. (For a full discussion of this campaign, see Hewitt.)

26. Harriet Linkin's rhetorical analysis of this story supports my reading, for she discerns in it two narrative voices that reveal a discrepancy between actual, unromantic military values and the romanticized understanding of military life that one might construct from reading Walter Scott and other chivalric authors. Specifically, Linkin points out that the first and last of the story's three sections, which depict Farquhar's hanging, are narrated by a brisk, distant, and merciless voice—the true military one, whereas the middle section, which presents the Union spy's duping of Farquhar, is told in a voice that partakes of the "glittering generalities that constitute Farquhar's own rhetorical code, . . . the chivalric code of the South" (143–44). It is this code that blinds Farquhar to the realities of military life and war and thus impels him to succumb to "the tempting glory offered by the Confederacy" (150).

27. Only after he has developed this scene of shock does Bierce orient his reader by sketching in a few details of the larger context, briefly explaining the Union and Confederate movements that led up to the Federals' being taken unawares.

28. In the short story "The Coup de Grâce," Bierce gives another reason besides ir-

revocable disorientation for an officer not to bother considering the prescriptions of regulations: they are ludicrously inadequate to the realities of the situation. While in *Miss Ravenel's Conversion* De Forest has Colburne simply rest content with the idea that the wounded must wait until after the battle for assistance, Bierce's narrator in "Coup" looks more closely and more questioningly at the actual effects of this regulation. This narrator reports that at the close of an unnamed battle, "[m]ost of the wounded had died of neglect while the right to minister to their wants was in dispute. It is an army regulation that the wounded must wait; the best way to care for them is to win the battle. It must be confessed that victory is a distinct advantage to a man requiring attention, but many do not live to avail themselves of it" (154).

Chapter 7. To March toward the Sound of the Guns

1. Bierce's preoccupation with this image very likely stems from his having encountered it firsthand early in his military career. In the memoir "On a Mountain," Bierce describes his initial brushes with battle in West Virginia in the autumn of 1861. His first encounter with the reality of combat occurs, he says, when his column, advancing to the attack, passes a number of corpses of Union soldiers killed earlier in the day. Their appearance is gruesome enough as it is—Bierce notes "yellow-clay faces," "blank, staring eyes," and "teeth uncovered by contraction of the lips" (8)—but it takes on an even more ghastly cast the next day, as Bierce and his now beaten and downcast comrades re-pass the spot. With characteristically vicious but understated irony that builds as the description continues, Bierce says he is surprised to observe that

   > these bodies had altered their positions. They appeared also to have thrown off some of their clothing, which lay near by, in disorder. Their expression, too, had an added blankness—they had no faces.
   >
   > As soon as the head of our straggling column had reached the spot a desultory firing had begun. One might have thought the living paid honors to the dead. No; the firing was a military execution; the condemned, a herd of galloping swine. They had eaten our fallen, but—touching magnanimity!—we did not eat theirs. (8–9)

2. One might argue that history itself is not to blame for Graffenreid's downfall but rather the character's acquisition of only a partial view of history, since the captain seems to have retained only a vision of supposedly heroic Roman individualism rather than the lessons of group responsibilities and interdependence that history can and does teach in De Forest's works. The previous chapter makes

clear, however, that in Bierce's view there can be no history that itself offers any more than a partial view.

3. M. E. Grenander connects this story to Bierce's recounting, in the 14 July 1883 issue of the *Wasp,* of his conduct as a one-man reconnaissance force at the battle of Nashville. Like the officer in "A Son of the Gods," as Grenander points out, Bierce preempted his commander's dispatch of a body of men to discover if a Confederate ambush lay ahead by volunteering to make this advance alone, thereby reducing the potential loss to just one life rather than a larger number. Grenander quotes Bierce's description of his behavior and notes its marked similarities to that of the "Son of the Gods" officer, particularly the passage in which Bierce reports that he "'dashed forward through every open space, into every suspicious looking wood, and spurred to the crest of every hill, exposing myself recklessly to draw the Confederate fire and disclose their position'" (119). The primary difference between this recollection and "A Son of the Gods," as Grenander says, is that in Bierce's memoir the foolhardy gesture reveals that there was no Confederate ambush, with the result that Bierce returned safely and treats his escapade as humorously misguided, whereas in the short story the officer's actions lead to his own and many other deaths and thus are presented as simultaneously heroic and tragic.

4. As noted in this study's second chapter, Marshall says of men under fire that "[t]he majority are unwilling to take extraordinary risks and do not aspire to a hero's role," but he qualifies this assertion with the insight that one of the primary spurs to extraordinarily courageous actions is that the majority "are equally unwilling that they should be considered the least worthy among those present" (149).

5. Whether "vain devotion" here refers to the conduct of the officer or that of the men who seek to avenge him, or perhaps to both, is a question Bierce leaves the reader to ponder.

6. For a full account of this battle, see Cleaves; Lamers; and McWhiney.

7. That this existentialist approach offers only a chance of survival, not a guarantee, is evident in two of Bierce's stories in which the protagonists consciously choose to focus on their immediate duty to the exclusion of all other concerns and come to grief as a result. "One Kind of Officer" tells the story of Union artillery Captain Ransome, who at the opening of the story is smarting under a dressing-down from his brigade commander, General Cameron, for an earlier questioning of Cameron's orders. "'[I]t is not permitted to you to know anything,'" Cameron shouts. "'It is sufficient that you obey my order—which permit me to repeat. If you perceive any movement of troops in your front you are to open fire'" (193). Stung by Cameron's harshness, Ransome obeys this order to the letter: when a body of troops crosses the front of his battery a few mo-

ments later he directs the full force of his guns upon them and cuts them to pieces, despite his knowledge that these are Union men coming to reinforce his position. When the division commander, General Masterson, rides up and demands to know why Ransome knowingly fired on his fellows, Ransome informs Masterson that General Cameron gave the original order. For a moment Ransome secretly rejoices in what he believes to be his revenge upon his arrogant superior, but his triumph dissipates instantly when Masterson informs him that Cameron has just been killed in another part of the line and so cannot confirm his claim. The story ends with Ransome surrendering to the provost-marshal, knowing that his rigid focus on duty will place him in front of a firing squad before many more days pass.

"The Affair at Coulter's Notch" takes another Union artillery officer, Captain Coulter, for its protagonist. Ordered by his division commander, identified only as "the general," to engage his battery against a much larger force of retreating Confederate artillery, Coulter at first shows reluctance, evidently because a plantation house stands between the opposing forces, but then, as a dutiful soldier, obeys. In the ensuing duel, Coulter's battery is decimated and the house is severely battered, while the reader learns that the general bears Coulter a grudge as a result of an earlier contretemps between the general and Coulter's wife, an ardent secessionist. The meaning of this information only becomes clear at the story's end, when Union officers inspecting the cellar of the ruined house discover a powder-blackened man cradling in his arms a dead woman and dead child. This vision of horror is intensified by their realization that "[a] yard away, near an irregular depression in the beaten earth which formed the cellar's floor—a fresh excavation with a convex bit of iron, having jagged edges, visible in one of the sides—lay an infant's foot" (152). Stunned, one of the officers asks the begrimed figure what he is doing there. "'This house belongs to me, sir,'" is the response, after which the following dialogue concludes the story:

"'To you? Ah, I see! And these?'
"'My wife and child. I am Captain Coulter.'" (153)

8. The single possible exception to this statement, the one model for combat depictions Bierce seems to have regarded positively and drawn on, is, as noted in chapter 6, Hazen's memoir, which is itself a model for the rejection of conventional approaches in its use of multiple perspectives in presenting the battle at Pickett's Mill.

Works Cited

Aaron, Daniel. "Ambrose Bierce's Civil War." Davidson 170–81.
———. *The Unwritten War.* New York: Knopf, 1973.
Ahnebrink, Lars. *The Beginnings of Naturalism in American Fiction.* Cambridge: Harvard UP, 1950.
Averell, William. *Ten Years in the Saddle: The Memoir of William Woods Averell.* Ed. Edward K. Eckert and Nicholas J. Amato. San Francisco: Presidio, 1978.
Barthes, Roland. *Mythologies.* Trans. Annette Lavers. New York: Hill and Wang, 1972.
Becker, Stephen. "On John William De Forest's *Miss Ravenel's Conversion from Secession to Loyalty.*" *Classics of Civil War Fiction.* Ed. David Madden and Peggy Bach. Jackson: UP of Mississippi, 1991. 23–36.
Berkove, Lawrence I. "Arms and the Man: Ambrose Bierce's Response to War." *Michigan Academician* 1 (1969): 21–30.
———. Introduction. *Skepticism and Dissent: Selected Journalism from 1898–1901.* By Ambrose Bierce. i–xvii.
Bierce, Ambrose. "The Affair at Coulter's Notch." McCann 142–53.
———. "An Affair of Outposts." McCann 171–83.

———. "A Bivouac of the Dead." McCann 71–73.
———. "Chickamauga." McCann 99–107.
———. "The Coup de Grâce." McCann 154–61.
———. "The Crime at Pickett's Mill." McCann 38–49.
———. *The Devil's Dictionary.* 1911. New York: Dover, 1993.
———. "George Thurston." McCann 214–19.
———. "A Horseman in the Sky." McCann 77–85.
———. "Jupiter Doke, Brigadier-General." McCann 247–58.
———. "Killed at Resaca." McCann 133–41.
———. "A Little of Chickamauga." McCann 32–37.
———. "An Occurrence at Owl Creek Bridge." McCann 86–98.
———. "On a Mountain." McCann 3–9.
———. "One Kind of Officer." McCann 193–205.
———. "One of the Missing." McCann 117–32.
———. "One Officer, One Man." McCann 206–13.
———. "A Resumed Identity." McCann 239–46.
———. *Skepticism and Dissent: Selected Journalism from 1898–1901.* Ed. Lawrence I. Berkove. Ann Arbor: Delmas, 1980.
———. "A Son of the Gods." McCann 108–16.
———. "What I Saw of Shiloh." McCann 10–31.
———. "What Occurred at Franklin." McCann 62–70.
Blake, J. A. "The Organization as an Instrument of Violence." *Sociological Quarterly* 2.3 (1970): 330–54.
Bocca, Geoffrey. *Best Seller.* New York: Wyndham, 1981.
Brazil, John R. "Behind the Bitterness: Ambrose Bierce in Text and Context." *American Literary Realism* 13 (1980): 225–37.
Caesar, Julius. *War Commentaries of Caesar.* Trans. Rex Warner. New York: New American Library, 1960.
Clark, Champ. *Decoying the Yanks: Jackson's Valley Campaign.* Alexandria: Time-Life, 1984.
Cleaves, Freeman. *Rock of Chickamauga: The Life of General George H. Thomas.* Norman: U of Oklahoma P, 1948.
Couser, G. Thomas. "Writing the Civil War: Ambrose Bierce's 'Jupiter Doke, Brigadier-General.'" *Studies in American Fiction* 18 (1990): 87–98.
Cowie, Alexander. *The Rise of the American Novel.* New York: American Book, 1948.
Cox, Jacob D. *The Battle of Franklin, Tennessee: November 30, 1864.* New York: Scribner's, 1897.
———. *The March to the Sea: Franklin and Nashville.* New York: Scribner's, 1882.
Cox, Joseph T. Introduction. *The Written Wars: American War Prose Through the Civil*

War. Ed. Joseph T. Cox. New Haven, CT: Archon, 1996. xiii–xv.

Crane, Stephen. "War Memories." *Tales of War*. Vol. 6 of the University of Virginia Edition of *The Works of Stephen Crane*. Ed. Fredson Bowers. Charlottesville: UP of Virginia, 1970. 222–63. 10 vols.

Creasy, Edward S. *The Fifteen Decisive Battles of the World: From Marathon to Waterloo*. 1851. New York: Harper, 1878.

Croushore, James H. "Editor's Preface." *A Volunteer's Adventures*. By John William De Forest. xi–xii.

Davidson, Cathy N., ed. *Critical Essays on Ambrose Bierce*. Boston: G. K. Hall, 1982.

———. *The Experimental Fictions of Ambrose Bierce: Structuring the Ineffable*. Lincoln: U of Nebraska P, 1984.

Deamer, Robert Glen. *The Importance of Place in the American Literature of Hawthorne, Thoreau, Crane, Adams, and Faulkner*. New York: Edwin Mellen, 1990.

De Castro, Adolph. *Portrait of Ambrose Bierce*. 1929. New York: Beekman, 1974.

De Forest, John William. "Caesar's Art of War and of Writing." *Atlantic Monthly* Sept. 1879: 273–88.

———. "Farragut." *Atlantic Monthly* May 1880: 688–91.

———. "The First Time Under Fire." *Harper's New Monthly Magazine* Sept. 1864: 475–82.

———. "The Great American Novel." *Nation* 9 Jan. 1868: 27–29.

———. "Letter to Howells." *Harper's New Monthly Magazine* May 1877: 987.

———. *Miss Ravenel's Conversion from Secession to Loyalty*. 1867. Ed. Gordon S. Haight. San Francisco: Rinehart, 1955.

———. "Our Military Past and Future." *Atlantic Monthly* Nov. 1879: 561–75.

———. *Poems: Medley and Palestina*. New Haven: Tuttle, Morehouse and Taylor, 1902.

———. "Recent Literature." *Atlantic Monthly* Sept. 1879: 405–7.

———. *Seacliff; or The Mystery of the Westerveldts*. Boston: Phillips, Sampson, 1859.

———. *A Volunteer's Adventures*. Ed. James H. Croushore. New Haven: Yale UP, 1946.

de Man, Paul. *Blindness and Insight: Essays in the Rhetoric of Contemporary Criticism*. Minneapolis: U of Minnesota P, 1983.

Diffley, Kathleen. "The Roots of Tara: Making War Civil." *American Quarterly* 36 (1984): 359–72.

Dollard, John. *Fear in Battle*. New Haven: Yale UP, 1943.

Eagleton, Terry. *Literary Theory*. Minneapolis: U of Minnesota P, 1983.

Fatout, Paul. "Ambrose Bierce, Civil War Topographer." *American Literature* 26 (1954): 391–400.

———. *Ambrose Bierce: The Devil's Lexicographer*. Norman: U of Oklahoma P, 1951.

Frankel, Nat. *Patton's Best.* New York: Hawthorn, 1978.
Frederic, Harold. Rev. of *The Red Badge of Courage. New York Times* 29 Jan. 1896: 32.
Gargano, James W. Introduction. *Critical Essays on John William De Forest.* Ed. James W. Gargano. Boston: G. K. Hall, 1981. 5–27.
Grattan, C. Hartley. *Bitter Bierce: A Mystery of American Letters.* New York: Cooper Square, 1966.
Grenander, M. E. *Ambrose Bierce.* New York: Twayne, 1971.
Haight, Gordon S. Introduction. *Miss Ravenel's Conversion from Secession to Loyalty.* By John William De Forest. v–xx.
Haley, John W. *The Rebel Yell & the Yankee Hurrah: The Civil War Journal of a Maine Volunteer.* Ed. Ruth L. Silliker. Camden: Down East, 1985.
Hart, Basil H. Liddell. *Strategy: The Indirect Approach.* New York: Praeger, 1954.
Hay, Thomas R. *Hood's Tennessee Campaign.* Dayton, OH: Morningside, 1976.
Hewitt, Lawrence Lee. *Port Hudson: Confederate Bastion on the Mississippi.* Baton Rouge: Louisiana State UP, 1987.
Hijiya, James A. *J. W. De Forest and the Rise of American Gentility.* Hanover: UP of New England, 1988.
Holmes, Richard. *Acts of War.* New York: Free P, 1985.
Hood, John B. *Advance and Retreat: Personal Experiences in the United States and Confederate Armies.* Ed. Richard N. Current. Bloomington: Indiana UP, 1959.
Howells, William Dean. "The Editor's Study." *Harper's Monthly* May 1886: 973.
———. Rev. of *Miss Ravenel's Conversion from Secession to Loyalty. Atlantic Monthly* July 1867: 120–22.
James, William. *The Principles of Psychology.* Vol. 1. 1890. New York: Dover, 1950. 2 vols.
Jameson, Fredric. *The Political Unconscious: Narrative as a Socially Symbolic Act.* Ithaca: Cornell UP, 1981.
Keegan, John. *The Face of Battle.* New York: Vintage, 1977.
Keegan, John, and Richard Holmes. *Soldiers: A History of Men in Battle.* New York: Viking, 1986.
Kennedy, David. *Over Here: The First World War and American Society.* New York: Oxford UP, 1980.
Kinglake, Alexander. *The Invasion of the Crimea: Its Origin, and an Account of Its Progress down to the Death of Lord Raglan.* Vol. 4. Edinburgh: William Blackwood, 1868. 9 vols.
Kolb, Harold. *The Illusion of Life: American Realism as a Literary Form.* Charlottesville: UP of Virginia, 1969.
Lamers, William M. *The Edge of Glory: A Biography of General William S. Rosecrans, U.S.A.* New York: Harcourt, Brace, 1961.
Leisy, Ernest E. *The American Historical Novel.* Norman: U of Oklahoma P, 1950.
Levin, Harry. *The Gates of Horn.* New York: Oxford UP, 1963.

———. "What Is Realism?" *Comparative Literature* 3 (1951): 193–99.

Light, James F. *John William De Forest.* New York: Twayne, 1965.

Limon, John. *Writing After War: American War Fiction from Realism to Postmodernism.* New York: Oxford UP, 1994.

Linderman, Gerald F. *Embattled Courage: The Experience of Combat in the American Civil War.* New York: Free P, 1987.

Linkin, Harriet K. "Narrative Technique in 'An Occurrence at Owl Creek Bridge.'" *Journal of Narrative Technique* 18.2 (1988): 137–52.

Lively, Robert A. *Fiction Fights the Civil War.* Chapel Hill: U of North Carolina P, 1957.

Lundberg, David. "The American Literature of War: The Civil War, World War I, and World War II." *American Quarterly* 36 (1984): 373–88.

Madden, David, and Peggy Bach. Introduction. *Classics of Civil War Fiction* 3–22.

Marshall, S. L. A. *Island Victory.* 1945. Washington, D.C.: Zenger, 1982.

———. *Men Against Fire.* New York: William Morrow, 1947.

McCann, William. Introduction. McCann iii–xi.

———, ed. *Ambrose Bierce's Civil War.* Los Angeles: Gateway, 1956.

McDonough, James L. *Shiloh: In Hell Before Night.* Knoxville: U of Tennessee P, 1977.

McDonough, James L., and Thomas L. Connelly. *Five Tragic Hours: The Battle of Franklin.* Knoxville: U of Tennessee P, 1983.

McFeely, William S. *Grant: A Biography.* New York: Norton, 1981.

McMurry, Richard M. *John Bell Hood and the War for Southern Independence.* Lexington: UP of Kentucky, 1982.

McNerney, Brian C. "Responsibly Inventing History: An Interview with Tim O'Brien." *War, Literature, and the Arts* 6.2 (Fall/Winter 1994): 1–26.

McPherson, James M. *The Battle Cry of Freedom.* New York: Oxford UP, 1988.

———. *For Cause and Comrades: Why Men Fought in the Civil War.* New York: Oxford UP, 1997.

McWhiney, Grady. *Braxton Bragg and Confederate Defeat.* New York: Columbia UP, 1969.

Miller, Wayne Charles. *An Armed America: Its Face in Fiction—A History of the American Military Novel.* New York: New York UP, 1970.

Mitchell, Reid. *Civil War Soldiers: Their Expectations and Their Experiences.* New York: Viking, 1988.

Napier, William. *History of the War in the Peninsula.* Ed. Charles Stuart. Chicago: U of Chicago P, 1979.

Nolan, Alan T. *Lee Considered: General Robert E. Lee and Civil War History.* Chapel Hill: U of North Carolina P, 1991.

O'Brien, Tim. *The Things They Carried.* 1990. New York: Penguin, 1991.

O'Connor, Richard. *Ambrose Bierce: A Biography.* Boston: Little, Brown, 1967.

O'Donnell, Thomas F. "De Forest, Van Petten, and Stephen Crane." *American Literature* 27 (1956): 578–80.

Oviatt, Edwin. "J. W. De Forest in New Haven." *New York Times* 17 Dec. 1898: 856. Rpt. in *Critical Essays on John William De Forest*. 38–43.

Owen, Wilfred. *Collected Letters*. Ed. Harold Owen and John Bell. New York: Oxford UP, 1967.

Plutarch. *The Lives of the Noble Grecians and Romans*. Dryden translation. Chicago: Encyclopaedia Britannica, 1952.

Putnam, Jackson K. "Historical Fact and Literary Truth: The Problem of Authenticity in Western American Literature." *Western American Literature* 15 (1980): 17–23.

Rev. of *Miss Ravenel's Conversion from Secession to Loyalty*. *Harper's Monthly* Aug. 1867: 401.

Rev. of *Miss Ravenel's Conversion from Secession to Loyalty*. *Nation* 4 (20 Jun. 1867): 2.

Rev. of *Miss Ravenel's Conversion from Secession to Loyalty*. *New York Post* 21 May 1867: 1.

Robertson, James I., Jr. *Soldiers Blue and Gray*. Columbia: U of South Carolina P, 1988.

———. *Tenting Tonight: The Soldier's Life*. Alexandria: Time-Life, 1984.

Royster, Charles. *The Destructive War: William Tecumseh Sherman, Stonewall Jackson, and the Americans*. New York: Knopf, 1991.

Rutherford, Andrew. "Realism and the Heroic: Some Reflections on War Novels." *Yearbook of English Studies* 12 (1982): 194–207.

Scarry, Elaine. *The Body in Pain*. New York: Oxford UP, 1985.

Schama, Simon. *Dead Certainties (Unwarranted Speculations)*. New York: Knopf, 1991.

Smoler, Fredric. "The Secret of the Soldiers Who Didn't Shoot." *American Heritage* Mar. 1989: 37–45.

Solomon, Eric. "The Bitterness of Battle: Ambrose Bierce's War Fiction." Davidson 182–94.

———. Introduction. *The Faded Banners: A Treasury of Nineteenth-Century Civil War Fiction*. Ed. Eric Solomon. New York: Thomas Yoseloff, 1960. vii–xii.

———. "John William DeForest." *The Faded Banners* 192–93.

———. "The Novelist as Soldier: Cooke and DeForest." *American Literary Realism* 19.3 (1987): 80–88.

———. *Stephen Crane: From Parody to Realism*. Cambridge: Harvard UP, 1966.

Spiller, Robert E. *The Cycle of American Literature: An Essay in Historical Criticism*. New York: Macmillan, 1955.

Stendhal. *The Charterhouse of Parma*. Trans. Margaret R. B. Shaw. Baltimore: Penguin, 1958.

Stone, Albert E., Jr. "Best Novel of the Civil War." *American Heritage* June 1962: 84–88.

Stovall, Floyd. "The Decline of Romantic Idealism, 1855–1871." *Transitions in American Literary History.* Ed. Harry Hayden Clark. Durham: Duke UP, 1954. 315–78.
Sweet, Timothy. *Traces of War.* Baltimore: Johns Hopkins UP, 1990.
Sword, Wiley. *Shiloh: Bloody April.* New York: William Morrow, 1974.
Thackeray, William Makepeace. *The History of Henry Esmond.* 1852. Baltimore: Penguin, 1970.
———. *Vanity Fair.* 1848. Baltimore: Penguin, 1968.
Thompson, Lawrence S. "The Civil War in Fiction." *Civil War History* 2 (Mar. 1956): 83–95.
Wertheim, Stanley, and Paul Sorrentino. *The Crane Log.* New York: G. K. Hall, 1994.
White, Hayden. *The Content of the Form: Narrative Discourse and Historical Representation.* Baltimore: Johns Hopkins UP, 1987.
Whitman, Walt. *Specimen Days.* 1882. New York: New American Library, 1961.
Williams, Stanley T. Introduction. Croushore v–ix.
Wilson, Edmund. *Patriotic Gore.* 1962. Boston: Northeastern UP, 1984.
Wilt, Napier. "Ambrose Bierce and the Civil War." *American Literature* 1 (1929): 260–85.
Ziff, Larzer. *The American 1890s: Life and Times of a Lost Generation.* New York: Viking, 1966.

Index

Aaron, Daniel, 40, 42, 43, 123, 141n.2
Adams, William T., 23
Aeschylus, 146n.6
Ahnebrink, Lars, 66, 149n.2
Albuera, battle of, xi, 59
Alger, Horatio, 23
American Mercury, 124
Aristotle, 66
Atlantic Monthly, x, xi, 24, 35, 44, 143n.1, 145n.2
Averell, William, 16–17

Bach, Peggy, 141n.2
Balaclava, battle of, 55
Balzac, Honoré de, 40
Banks, Nathaniel, 72, 155n.25

Barthes, Roland, 71
Bartlett, Asa W., 6
Battle, heroism in, 92, 153n.19; nature of, xiv, 43, 134–35, 138–40; soldiers' behavior in, xiv, 57; soldiers' fears in, xiv, 4–5, 8–14, 143n.1; soldiers' motivations in, 4–5, 142n.1, 157n.4; soldiers' response to, 138–40; soldiers' understanding of, 4, 37–38, 42; *see also* Bierce; De Forest
Battlefield, appearance of, 3–4, 42; *see also* De Forest
Battles and Leaders of the Civil War, 153n.17
Becker, Stephen, 132, 144n
Berkove, Lawrence, 99, 124, 126
Bierce, Albert, 124
Bierce, Ambrose, x, 92, 140, 142n.2; on

Bierce, Ambrose, *cont.*
Buell, 82–83, 150n.8; on chivalry, 107, 116–17; on civilians' response to battle, 98–99; continuing relevance of, 131–35; on Crane, 148n.1; on editors, 154n.21; and existentialism, 126, 129–30, 132, 134, 157n.7; on Grant, 82–83, 84, 150n.8; on Hazen, 84, 87; on heroism, 93, 95, 97, 119–20, 121, 127, 129; on Howard, 85, 90–91, 151n.10; on Johnston, 87–89; literary influences on, 65–66, 90, 123, 130, 149n.2, 153n.17, 158n.8; as literary stylist, 102, 154n.24, 155n.26; military career of, 79, 151n.11, 157n.3; on military professionalism, 132; on military training, 80–81; narrative technique of, 87–90, 93, 100, 116–17, 152n.15, 155n.27; on nature of battle, 73, 99–100, 103–6, 121–23, 132, 136, 156n.1; on realism in battle writing, 66, 78, 79–80, 81, 83, 84–86, 89, 100, 126–27, 150n.9; as realist, xiv–xv, 15–19, 73–79, 101–2, 133–35, 149n.5; response to battle of, 76–77, 78, 100, 101, 123–26, 136, 138, 150n.6; on responsibilities of officers, 77, 127, 156n.28; on Sheridan, 84; on Sherman, 82–83, 84, 85; similarities and differences between writings of and De Forest's, 73, 74–79, 81, 100–102, 112, 127–28, 130, 131–32; on soldiers' behavior in battle, 74–76, 103–6, 107–10, 111–12, 113–15, 117–22, 126–27; on soldiers' fears in battle, 109–10; soldiers' motivations in battle, 128; on soldiers' understanding of battle, 73–74, 81, 85–86, 100–101, 114, 115–16, 151n.11, 154n.23; on value of history, 78–79, 80–81, 83–85, 89, 90–91, 95, 97–99, 105–6, 110–11, 112–13, 115, 118, 120–22, 127, 130, 132, 156n.2
—*Works:* "Affair at Coulter's Notch, The," 158n.7; "Affair of Outposts, An," 98, 150n.8; "Bivouac of the Dead, A," 84; "Chickamauga," 16, 17, 98–99, 103, 119; "Coup de Grâce, The," 84, 104, 155n.28; "Crime at Pickett's Mill, The," 73–76, 84–90, 92, 97, 100, 105, 152n.13, 155n.25, 158n.8; *Devil's Dictionary, The,* 78, 81, 154n.21; "George Thurston," 104–5, 151n.11; "Horseman in the Sky, A," 103–4; "Jupiter Doke, Brigadier-General," 84, 92–97, 99, 103, 113, 152n.13, 154n.20, 155n.25; "Killed at Resaca," 122–23; "Little of Chickamauga, A," 128–29, 152n.13, 153n.17; "Occurrence at Owl Creek Bridge, An," 98, 103, 149n.2, 155n.26; "On a Mountain," 156n.1; "One Kind of Officer," 113–14, 157n.7; "One of the Missing," 104, 149n.2; "One Officer, One Man," 106–13, 114, 115, 121, 156n.2; "Resumed Identity, A," 125, 136; "Son of the Gods, A," 115–21, 122, 128, 157n.3, 157n.5; "What I Saw of Shiloh," 77, 100–102, 105, 127, 150n.8, 152n.13, 153n.17; "What Occurred at Franklin," 81–82, 153n.17

Blake, J. A., 38
Bonaparte, Napoleon, 43
Boyd, Cyrus, 140
Brazil, John R., 124
Buell, Don Carlos, 82–83, 91; *see also* Bierce

Caesar, Julius, 35, 43, 45–47, 50–54, 55, 56, 57, 58, 59, 60, 61, 62, 67, 146n.1, 147n.2; *see also* De Forest
Carlyle, Thomas, 43
Catch-22 (Heller), 83, 92
Cedar Creek, battle of, 44, 70, 147n.4
Chancellorsville, battle of, 6, 143n.2
Cheatham, Benjamin, 82, 150n.7
Chickamauga, battle of, 99, 128–29

Child, Lydia, 23
Churchill, Winston, 147n.3
Civil War, American, ix, 80; accounts of battle in, xv, 11–12, 135; heroism in, 92; literature of, 19, 135–36, 141n.2, 144n; nature of battle in, 5–7, 142n.2, 149n.4
Civil War, Spanish, 5
Clark, Champ, 7
Commentaries (Caesar), 44, 45–47, 50–54, 58, 61, 147n.2, 147n.4; *see also* De Forest
Cooke, John Esten, 23
Cooper, James Fenimore, 40
Coppola, Francis Ford, 133
Couser, G. Thomas, 87, 152n.13, 154n.20, 154n.22, 154n.24
Cowie, Alexander, 143n.1
Cox, Joseph T., 143n.1
Crane, Stephen, ix, 15, 19, 127, 135, 148n.5; *see also* Bierce
Creasy, Edward, 33, 142n.3, 146n.6, 146n.7
Crotty, Daniel, 37
Croushore, James H., 146n.4, 147n.4
Cummings, E. E., 39

Davidson, Cathy, 92, 105–6, 121, 134
Davis, Robert H., 149n.1
Deamer, Robert Glen, 127
De Forest, John William, x, 6, 65, 79, 83, 140, 142n.2; on appearance of battlefield, 30–31; continuing relevance of, 131–35; on heroism, 73, 127; ideology of, 66–68, 72; on Julius Caesar, 44–45, 49, 52–53, 59, 61, 66, 70, 133, 147n.2, 148n.7; literary influences on, 40–41, 42–43, 44–45, 49, 54–55, 57–58, 60–62, 130, 149n.2; as literary stylist, 58–62, 101–2, 143n.1, 148n.5; military career of, 36, 62, 147n.4, 148n.6; on military professionalism, 132; on military training, 24–25, 28, 81, 145n.2, 145n.3; and mythology, 70–71; narrative technique of, 86, 100, 147n.4; on nature of battle, 26, 100, 102, 132, 136, 137, 149n.4; on realism in battle writing, x–xi, 24–27, 35–36, 43, 45, 50, 66, 102, 137; as realist, xiv–xv, 15–19, 23–24, 27–28, 31–32, 33–35, 40–41, 47–50, 67, 75, 101–2, 132–35, 143n.1, 144n, 145n.1; response to battle of, 29–30, 31, 69, 76–77, 78, 136–38; on responsibilities of officers, 68–69, 72–73, 77, 101, 127, 156n.28; similarities and differences between writings of and Bierce's, 73, 74–79, 81, 100–102, 112, 127–28, 130, 131–32; on soldiers' behavior in battle, 25–26, 30–31, 32, 35, 48–49, 67–68, 71, 74, 127, 149n.3; on soldiers' fears in battle, 30, 71, 72–73; on soldiers' motivations in battle, 127–28; on soldiers' understanding of battle, 73, 86; on Tacitus, 35, 44, 53, 133; on Tolstoy, 71; on value of history, 68–70, 72–73, 78–79, 100, 102, 127, 130, 132, 154n.25

—*Works:* "Caesar's Art of War and of Writing," 44, 53, 61, 62, 65, 145n.2, 148n.7; "First Time Under Fire, The," 27–35, 60, 68–69, 70, 75, 76, 86, 100, 101–2, 127, 146n.5, 147n.4, 150n.6; "Great American Novel, The," 37; *Medley and Palestina,* 36; *Miss Ravenel's Conversion from Secession to Loyalty,* 15–16, 23–24, 35, 36, 40, 43, 44, 47–50, 55, 60–61, 68, 70, 71, 72, 75, 100, 128, 132, 134, 136–38, 143n.1, 144n, 145n.1, 154n.25, 156n.28; "Our Military Past and Future," x, 24–27, 28, 35, 39, 43, 45, 50, 55, 65, 67, 72, 74, 75, 81; "Recent Literature," 31; *Seacliff, or, The Mystery of the Westerveldts,* 36, 40; *Volunteer's Adventures, A,* x, 16, 27, 36, 37, 58, 68, 70, 72, 100, 137, 146n.4, 146n.5, 147n.4; *Witching Times,* 36

de Man, Paul, 91
Dickens, Charles, 40
Diffley, Kathleen, 39
Dollard, John, 5, 9, 10–11, 29, 30, 142n.1
Dos Passos, John, 39
Du Picq, Ardant, 11, 13, 25

Eagleton, Terry, 67
Early, Jubal, 70
Eggleston, George Cary, 142n.2
Eliot, George, 40

Face of Battle, The (Keegan), xi
Falklands War, 139
Farragut, David, 145n.2
Farragut, Loyall, 145n.2
Fatout, Paul, 124–25, 128, 152n.11, 153n.16
Frankel, Nat, 38
Franklin, battle of, 81–82, 150n.7
Frederic, Harold, 19, 41, 62, 65
French and Indian War, 153n.19
Freud, Sigmund, 9
Froude, James A., 35

Galaxy, 146n.4
Gargano, James W., 143n.1
Gettysburg, battle of, 12
Gilmore, James Roberts, 23
Grant, Ulysses, 82–83, 91, 92, 95, 99, 154n.20, 155n.25; *see also* Bierce
Grattan, Hartley, 66
Grenander, Mary E., 119, 126, 131, 157n.3

Haight, Gordon, 40, 42, 43
Haley, John, 12–13
Hannibal, 70
Harper's New Monthly Magazine, 23, 27, 71, 143n.1, 146n.4, 146n.5

Hart, Basil Liddell, 37
Hasford, Gustav, 133
Hazen, William B., 65, 84, 89, 90, 91, 92, 125, 151n.10, 153n.16, 153n.17, 158n.8; *see also* Bierce
Hearst, William Randolph, 79
Heller, Joseph, 83
Hemingway, Ernest, 39, 127, 148n.5
Herr, Michael, 133
Hijiya, James A., 144n, 148n.6, 148n.7
History of the War in the Peninsula, A (Napier), xi
Holmes, Oliver Wendell, Jr., 37
Holmes, Richard, 3–4, 8, 9, 10, 26, 36, 37, 39, 138, 139
Hood, John Bell, 82, 87, 90, 150n.7
Hooker, Joseph, 143n.2, 154n.20
Hosmer, James Kendall, x
Howard, O. O., 65, 75, 87, 88, 89, 90, 91, 92, 99; *see also* Bierce
Howells, William Dean, x, 17, 18, 67, 71, 72, 79, 86, 132, 143n.1

Iliad, The (Homer), 66, 86
Invasion of the Crimea, The (Kinglake), 43, 55

Jackson, Thomas J. ("Stonewall"), 7, 92, 153n.18
James, Henry, 18
James, William, 143n.1
Jameson, Fredric, 91
Johnston, Albert Sidney, 146n.7
Johnston, Joseph E., 87–90, 152n.14; *see also* Bierce

Keegan, John, xi–xiv, xv, 8, 11, 25, 39, 43, 45–47, 50, 51, 53, 54, 58, 59, 79, 142n.3, 146n.1

Kennedy, David, 39–40
Kennesaw Mountain, battle of, 79, 104, 124
Kinglake, Alexander, 43, 54–61, 62, 147n.3
Kipling, Rudyard, 147n.3
Kirkland, Joseph, x, 142n.2
Kolb, Harold, 144n.1
Kubrick, Stanley, 133

Labadieville, battle of, 28
Lanier, Sidney, x, 142n.2
Lee, Robert E., 92, 143n.2
Leisy, Ernest, 145n.1
Levin, Harry, 18, 19
Limon, John, 134, 141n.2, 144n
Linderman, Gerald, 5–7, 25, 37
Linkin, Harriet, 155n.26
Lively, Robert A., 141n.2
Lundberg, David, 39–40, 135–36, 138

Madden, David, 141n.2
Malvern Hill, battle of, 16
Marathon, battle of, 33, 146n.6
Marshall, S. L. A., 9, 10, 13–14, 25, 30, 37–38, 39, 113, 115, 143n.1, 145n.3, 152n.15, 157n.4
McCann, William, 150n.5
McPherson, James, 142n.1, 142n.2
Mencken, H. L., 149n.5
Mexican War, 5–6
Miles, Nelson, 80
Miller, Wayne, x, 141n.2
Murat, Joachim, 128

Napier, William, xi–xiii, xiv, 35, 43, 59–60, 61, 142n.3
New Orleans State, 136
New York Journal, 148n.1
New York Post, 143n.1
New York Press, 149n.1

New York Times, 36
Nolan, Alan T., 92, 93

O'Brien, Tim, 36–37, 133–35, 139–40, 146n.3
O'Connor, Richard, 76, 149n.5, 154n.20
O'Donnell, Thomas F., 62
Oviatt, Edwin, 36, 40, 62
Owen, Wilfred, 138–39

Patton, George, 8
Pharsalia, battle of, 49–52, 53
Plutarch, 147n.2
Pollard, Percival, 148n.1
Port Hudson, siege of, 15–16, 68, 72, 73, 100, 135, 155n.25
Putnam, Jackson K., 17, 18, 67

Realism in battle writing, ix–xv, 3, 4, 5, 19, 36–40, 132–40; language and, 38–39; role of personal experience in, 38; role of reading in, 39–41; *see also* Bierce; De Forest
Realism as literary movement, x, 17–18
Red Badge of Courage, The (Crane), 19, 145n.1; *see also* Bierce
Robertson, James I., Jr., 7
Rosecrans, William, 129
Royster, Charles, 92, 93, 153n.18
Rutherford, Andrew, 132–33

Salamis, battle of, 33, 146n.6
San Francisco Examiner, 79, 80, 82, 90, 126, 127, 128, 150n.6, 150n.9, 153n.16
Sargent, H. H., 151n.9
Scarry, Elaine, 77–78, 97
Schama, Simon, 92, 93, 153n.19
Scott, Walter, 40, 66, 144n, 155n.26
Sedgwick, John, 143n.2

Sheridan, Philip, 70, 147n.4; *see also* Bierce
Sherman, William T., 65, 82–83, 87, 88, 89, 90, 91, 92, 104; *see also* Bierce
Shiloh, battle of, 82–83, 92, 95, 98, 102, 146n.7, 150n.6, 150n.8
Smoler, Fredric, 143n.1
Solomon, Eric, 40, 65, 71, 73, 123, 142n.1, 144n, 149n.5
Sorrentino, Paul, 148n.1
Spanish-American War, ix, 79, 80, 126, 128, 151n.9
Spiller, Robert, 18
Steinmetz, Lee, 39
Stendhal, 40, 42–43, 144n, 149n.2
Sterling, George, 124
Stone, Albert E., Jr., 23, 61, 148n.5
Stone, Oliver, 133
Stovall, Floyd, 145n.1
Sweet, Timothy, 86

Thackeray, William Makepeace, 40, 43, 144n, 149n.2
Thomas, George, 129
Thompson, Lawrence, 145n.1
Tolstoy, Leo, 66, 144n, 149n.2; *see also* De Forest

Trowbridge, John Townsend, 23

Vanity Fair (Thackeray), 66, 144n; *see also* Thackeray
Vietnam War, 133, 139

Waterloo, battle of, 42
War and Peace (Tolstoy), 71, 149n.2; *see also* De Forest
Weitzel, Godfrey, 27–29, 33–34, 146n.7
Wertheim, Stanley, 148n.1
West, Benjamin, 153n.19
White, Hayden, 92, 93
Whitman, Walt, ix, 86–87, 141n.1, 152n.15
Williams, Stanley T., 36
Wilson, Edmund, 40, 42, 60, 141n.2, 145n.1
Wilt, Napier, 65, 89–90, 153n.17
Wolfe, James, 153n.19
World War I, 39–40

Ziff, Larzer, 65, 123, 125, 149n.5
Zola, Emile, 144n

Just What War Is was designed and typeset on a Macintosh computer system using PageMaker software. The text and titles are set in Adobe Garamond. This book was designed by Todd Duren, composed by Kimberly Scarbrough, and manufactured by Thomson-Shore, Inc. The recycled paper used in this book is designed for an effective life of at least three hundred years.

CH